THE ROAD TO DAYTONA

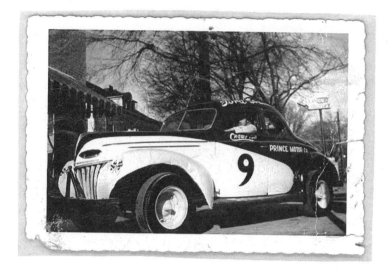

Produced and printed in U.S.A.

ISBN: 0-933078-16-1

Library of Congress Catalog Card Number: 86-92091

In Memory of John and Mary Brunner.
To know them was to love them.

TABLE OF CONTENTS

WORLD CHAMPIONSHIP STOCK CAR RACE - 1955!

There stood two young racing drivers from the relatively peaceful rural and suburban Carolinas on the shipping dock at Liverpool more than a little shaken as we faced two very serious inspectors from Scotland Yard.

I must quickly say, in all fairness to the memory of my friend, the late Bobby Myers, that he was the innocent victim of my escapade, if you can call it that. Bobby was with me on that dock for the very understandable, simple reason that he was tired of barnstorming Great Britain and he wanted to return home to the land of honeysuckle, grits and gravy and friendly sounds such as, "Welcome home, y'all!"

Let's go back a bit and properly set the scene for you.

Quickly stated, seven Southern stock car drivers were in England on a well-organized six months barnstorming racing schedule, arranged and conducted by American promoters Lester Vanadore and Buddy Davenport, in cooperation with a British promoter named Digger Pugh.

On the very first race day, the British promoter had shafted us, cheated us out of $4,800 which he had promised, but unfortunately and careless of us, was not in writing.

There was no choice but that we had to accept the fact that he had taken advantage of us, and for us to go on with the scheduled tour. The memory lingered on, however, especially in the back of my mind, because I had been the spokesman, that first day, for the seven racing musketeers.

A few months later, when the opportunity arose to work my own little 'sting' operation on Mr. Pugh, I seized the opportunity, and conned the rascal out of $3,500.

There was one more move which had to be made and that was for Bobby Myers and Curtis Crider to quickly board a ship leaving England for the good ole red, white and blue, stars and stripes U.S.A.

We could not say that we really feared for our lives, but knowing Mr. Pugh's reputation, there was good reason to want to avoid bodily pain and to keep all legs and arms without fractures, if you get the message.

Throughout the night following my last business transaction with Digger Pugh, Bobby and I darted and backtracked from subway to train to subway and more trains so as to stay out of sight after Pugh would learn the truth of the 'sting.'

We had made it to dockside at Liverpool where was berthed the HMS Britannia, loading for the trans-Atlantic trip to New York City.

Perhaps we could handle the street thugs who made up Pugh's goon squad, but we were now faced with a greater problem, two frightened young Americans looking into the eyes of two austere, no-nonsense men from Scotland Yard. We could only imagine the charges, undoubtedly exaggerated, that Pugh may have laid on us.

The inspectors from Scotland Yard had been instructed to apprehend us and stop us from boarding that ship. That is what they told us.

Although I was expecting Digger Pugh would make some move against us, this hit me quick and hard because we had been so close to escape.

Bobby and I had made it with great difficulty from London to Liverpool and we had our tickets in our pockets to get back to the United States.

We had lined up with the other passengers waiting to go through Customs. As we handed over our passports, the Customs man looked at them, then quietly said, "Mr. Crider and Mr. Myers, there is a man over there who wants to talk to you."

There was nothing to do but pull out of line and go over there and talk to the man from the Yard. In fact, there were two gentlemen from Scotland Yard, watching us carefully.

I told Bobby, "This hasn't anything to do with you and I'll straighten them out on that score and you can go on and get on this ship and go back to the States. I'll work it out myself, whatever. You go on home and don't worry about me. I'll keep in touch with you and will get home as soon as I can."

It is hard to believe that a couple of Southern stock car drivers could be involved with Scotland Yard inspectors.

* * *

It all began back in the early part of 1955, around January, perhaps early February, 32 years ago. Two auto racing promoters called me and six other racing drivers at the same time. They wanted seven American drivers to go to this one race promotion. That was their plan at the time. As mentioned, it later developed into a six-months long schedule.

It was Buddy Davenport who called me, a good friend of mine and a promoter of dirt track auto racing in the Carolinas.

In this proposed venture, Davenport was associated with Lester Vanadore, also a Carolinas race promoter.

Buddy asked me, "Do you want to go to London and race?"

I thought a minute and figured why not, I've raced everywhere else around the South, and I asked him, "What state is that in?"

Buddy said, "Oh, no. I mean downtown London, England."

I said, "Oh, come on, Buddy." He replied, "I'm not joking. Let me know something."

I happened to have a brand new car all fixed up. It was a '37 Ford with a modified '48 Ford engine and was getting ready for the 1955 season. "Of course I'll talk to you about it."

We had a meeting and the more we talked about it, the better it sounded. They had a good, straightforward salary deal for me. They would pay for shipping the car and me to England and home again.

Their plan was to pay me $100 a week plus all the prize money I earned because I would take my own race car. The other six fellows would be driving cars owned by Vanadore and Davenport, cars which the two promoters would buy

— 3 —

from people like Buddy Shuman and other Southern race car builders.

Because the other drivers had no car expense, they would get $50 a week. They would each keep half of any prize money they earned at each race.

If this sounds like low pay, remember it was 32 years ago and the cost of living was much lower than today.

To me, it seemed to be another adventure to go through, something like that. I was very, very interested in it. The only problem with it was some of the stories we had heard in the month or two it took to get ready to go, with passports, inoculations and all that good stuff.

Stock car racing was relatively new in England and we had heard that they ran in the opposite direction on the race track, turning right instead of left. That did give us cause for concern.

We finally got everything ready and had the seven drivers all lined up. They were Bobby Schuyler, Bill Irick and me from South Carolina; Neil 'Soapy' Castles and Bobby Myers from North Carolina; Lewis 'Possum' Jones and Pete Folse from the Tampa area of Florida.

Actually, Glenn 'Fireball' Roberts had been scheduled as one of the drivers, but because of a schedule conflict with his regular Fish Carburetor-owned Grand National ride, Roberts had to cancel. He was replaced by Bobby Myers. Bobby drove a '34 Ford which had been built for Fireball by Shuman and Willie Thompson in Charlotte.

There were no mechanics, no crews along. I guess I was the best mechanic of the bunch. Like Fireball, the others were all knowledgeable about chassis and engines, but they were basically drivers, while I usually built and maintained my race cars.

The plan was that all of us would help each other maintain the cars and that did work out well, very good, very little bitching or finger pointing.

As for spare parts, I loaded my car with everything I had, even used stuff and whatever. Loaded, it must have weighed as much as a Sherman tank.

Davenport was supposed to take along spare parts for the six cars they owned. I had given him a list of parts and equipment he would need.

Vanadore and Davenport made the arrangements, but all of us worked to load the cars and equipment and our clothes to be trucked up to New York City. To use the cliche, there were no chiefs. We were all Indians. Everybody worked together. There were no prima donnas.

Racing from week to week on the dirt tracks of the South - bullrings, some folks called them - was more or less routine, but this was to be an adventure. We were going to see how folks across the ocean raced, and we were going to race with them and against them.

We were cocky (at least confident that we would blow off their doors with little trouble). After all, we were the ones who had developed the technique of short track stock car racing, Southern style.

Of course, Vanadore and Davenport had journeyed down to Daytona Beach to make peace with the NASCAR folks, Big Bill France and Pat Purcell.

The overseas tour was not to be officially sanctioned by NASCAR, but we did have the approval and good wishes of France and Purcell. Actually, I doubt that they took this venture very seriously. They certainly did not appreciate the scope of what it turned out to be.

Don O'Reilly was then director of the NASCAR News Bureau and he doesn't recall ever writing a news story about the trip to England, "probably because it was not an official NASCAR event."

For us, however, it was a vastly different feeling as the caravan of tow cars and trailers and race cars left Charlotte, N.C., headed for New York harbor and the Queen Mary.

I want to tell you that it was one beautiful trip on that fine ship, really out of this world, especially for a South Carolina country boy. Everyone should have the opportunity, at least once, to travel on a luxury ocean liner. A whole new world of experience.

When we arrived at Southampton, England, we were surprised to be met by a delegation of British racing drivers. They had even brought their trucks to the Southampton docks to pick up our race cars and gear and transport it all up to London, where we were going to make our headquarters for the tour.

The guys were just great. They accepted us right from the beginning, but they did make many comments about our race cars as the machines were unloaded.

The fact that they seemed to be bewildered about our type of race car surprised us. We were to learn later that our cars were very lightweight according to their standards.

They examined the engines of our race cars, with three carburetors practically standard in the U.S., and the other equipment which we felt was quite normal.

Some of the British appeared to marvel at our equipment, others shook their heads in doubt.

They said they could not understand how we could keep such a light race car on a short track. They had only started racing stock cars in England a few years. Folks in the States had been engaged in that occupation for some 40 years, at various levels, of course.

Before our tour was over, the fellows from England were changing their cars quite a bit, after they saw how well our techniques worked. American stock car racing know-how had been imported to Britain, racer to racer.

The dock workers were rushing us to get the race cars off the ship and onto the trucks and move them out, but we all did manage to get acquainted and the Brits just wouldn't be hurried until they had looked over the race cars. After all, we were the new competition and no matter the nationality, racers will always be racers.

Before too long, we did get the race cars and gear trucked up to London from Southampton. The American promoters, Lester Vanadore and Buddy Davenport, with the assistance of the British promoter, Digger Pugh, had obtained the use, for us, of a big old garage there.

The English drivers and their crews really liked the powerful sounds of our modified engines as the race cars were driven onto the trucks at dockside, and later off the trucks at the London garage.

While the English were very curious about our cars and us, we also had many questions, because we had no idea what was awaiting us.

During the ride to London, the first thing I asked was in what direction did they race, and they said they turned left, just as we did back home. That was one big worry off our minds, because our cars were set up to run counterclockwise.

We would have had to make many steering and chassis changes if they had raced the other way, as the rumors had it back home.

Today, I marvel at the changes which have been made in the 32 years since we went to England, changes in race cars, changes in speedway construction and layout, and changes in dollars earned.

In England, on top of my $100 a week salary, I was earning from $100 to $300 a race, about the same as it was in the States in those days.

As for the race tracks, in the '50s, all our speedways were ovals, some short, some longer, and they were mostly dirt, but some were paved.

We did not realize it, that first day and evening in London, how simple it was for us, but you can be assured we had been worried and we were now relieved that we would be racing on all left turn ovals.

We got along fine with almost all the English drivers, but two were especially friendly, Pete Tucker and Johnny Brice.

In 1956, Johnny Brice sent me a Christmas card which was addressed simply:

Crawfish Crider
South Carolina, USA

Believe it or not, that card was delivered to my home in Abbeville, S.C.

You remember that U.S. Postal Service slogan, "Neither rain, nor snow, nor sleet, nor incomplete addresses . . . "

To show how friendships can last and last, until 1984, 29 years later, Pete Tucker and his wife, with their son Steve and his wife, and Pete's grandkids, continued to come to the States, almost every year, usually for the Daytona 500 and February Speed Weeks.

They would always visit me at our home in Ormond Beach, and we would go out on the town and have great times. It's a lovely family.

Although they haven't visited here the past couple of years, we still hear from them, keeping in touch by letters and Christmas cards.

Johnny Brice was one of the leading drivers over there and during those months in '55 he would take us out to his place in the country, his farm, and we just had a great time with them on and off the race tracks.

I give you these word pictures so that you, the racing fan, can better understand the real people behind the facade of the racer you see on the track.

They come in all shapes and sizes, various ethnic and religious backgrounds. Some are agreeable, generous, aggressive, docile, young, old, in between, rough talking, pleasant speaking, family men and playboys.

The point is that the makeup of the worldwide community called racers is little different than you will find downtown on a busy weekday, in a major shopping mall a few days before Christmas or on the beach or at the state fair any weekend - diverse.

There is one unifying link, they all have their private lives away from the speedways.

At the race tracks, Johnny Brice had a very nice setup on the Ford flathead engine, an Ardun overhead valve conversion.

In those days, with the Ardun unit, a fellow would use the standard flathead blocks and pistons, mount the Ardun unit and presto, a V8 overhead valve engine, more horsepower, more torque, wide continuous operating range, low fuel consumption, low first cost and low maintenance cost.

When completed, the Ardun conversion sported two carburetors and, in fact, looked like the Chrysler hemi engine which so dominated NASCAR Grand National racing later.

Don't let anyone tell you the Ardun conversion wouldn't bring one of those Ford blocks alive. It put a lot of power into that engine.

As mentioned, the first time I ever saw an Ardun conversion was in London, England, but it was designed, engineered and manufactured in New York City by a pair of ingenious brothers.

Don O'Reilly recalls visiting the Ardun Engine Co., Inc., in an industrial loft building at 503 West 56th Street in Manhattan, a short distance from the Henry Hudson Hotel, which was the favorite of so many auto racers in the late '40s and the '50s. O'Reilly visited Ardun to do an article for Speed

Age magazine about this Ardun setup which was causing such excitement along pit roads.

The creator was a fellow named Zora Arkus-Duntov, a very genial fellow who later went to work for General Motors engineering.

With his Ardun Ford conversion, Johnny Brice was one of the guys we had to beat every race during those months in England in 1955. Pete Tucker was tough on the race track too, both because of his equipment and his driving ability.

The first race was near London at Herringway Stadium at Wood Green. We were all keyed up. We had never been in competition against these guys before and there were many things unknown.

As mentioned, this first race was heavily promoted as a world championship. The British promoters had previously brought in seven drivers from other countries, and the British lads had beaten them all.

All that remained was this big race against the Yanks and the Brits would be the world champs of short track stock car racing.

We had never even practiced against them, although they did open the track the day before the race, so we could check out our own cars and their race track.

Digger Pugh, Vanadore and Davenport pulled out all the stops when it came to promotion. They had television crews on hand at the stadium and did we ever cooperate. After all, the seven of us were supposed to be partners in a way, getting a little piece of the action if we pulled in a capacity crowd. More on that later.

It was great to watch it later on British television because the seven of us would go down into a corner and just peel off like you see airplanes do at shows, and we would cross up the cars and slide through the corners.

We raced beside one another, then nose to tail, roaring down the backstretch. You've heard the broadcasters' cliche, "Door handle to door handle" even though race cars do not have any door handles. We did it.

It was impressive when it aired the night before the race and the broadcasters did their part, excitedly visualizing the confrontation when the visiting American drivers would meet the local Britishers.

The Digger Pugh hype was along the lines of our NFL Super Bowl, Saturday before the Daytona 500, Florence, S.C., before the Darlington Southern 500 and Indianapolis before that grand Memorial Sunday Hoosier classic.

Because of the world championship concept of this first race, the scoring was on a team basis. So many points to win, so many for second and so on.

If one of our drivers was the winner, another finished last, 14th, and others scattered near the front, we could win the championship. Also, they would pay money for only the first five places. In our case it made no difference, as it happened, because the American drivers took enough points to win.

Our success was mostly because the British drivers had not then gotten into the techniques of power sliding on dirt, and driving the cars through the corners as we were so used to doing back in the United States.

The British would more or less run down the straights and then motor around the turns. Their cars were quite a bit heavier because they were used to hitting each other, much more fender banging than did we. With our cars lighter, we avoided contact with each other and especially stayed away from them.

We had the advantage at the beginning, but I knew it wouldn't be long before they would lighten up their cars and adapt to our style of short track dirt track racing. Banking the cars into the corners, going in sideways, the rear end almost 180 degrees, and keeping the power on for a controlled slide.

Some folks will remember Curtis Turner was the outstanding master of the dirt track broadslide. Even without Turner as a model, I knew it wouldn't be long before they caught on to the quick way around a short track.

Bobby Myers was the winner of that first race and I had the pleasure of following him in second place. The Yanks were the undisputed world champs, London short track stock car racing style.

The Brits had beaten the French, Germans and Australians, and now we had vanquished the winners to that time.

There were photographers galore, newspaper and television, plus reporters and celebrities. Of course, we did not know who were the celebrities, but it was great, a big time for them, a big time for stock car racing and for us.

The reporters and the celebrities were asking questions and they were really interested in the invading Yankee drivers who were so good and who had beaten their home country stars. Stock car racing was new to them. Of course, for many, many years they had been accustomed to the Formula One Grand Prix racing and the other classes of open wheel, open cockpit, road racing cars and drivers, greats such as Stirling Moss and Juan Manuel Fangio and Mike Hawthorn.

Then the officials brought to what we would call victory lane a lady who was designated Miss Great Britain or some such title. She was a beauty, and obviously everyone's darling there in London town, a very popular beauty queen.

We didn't know it then, but such activities are handled a bit differently in staid Britain.

They had positioned race winner Bobby Myers standing on the race track side of the guard rail and the beauty queen, whose name was Sabrina, on the other side. The guard rail was about two and a half feet wide, perhaps the same height.

There was conversation and the young lady presented the trophy to Bobby.

Myers reacted as he would at a race track in the United States, only to learn they did not do things that way in

England in those days. Bobby handed his trophy to someone standing nearby and he reached across the guard rail and grabbed the young lady and put an old fashioned lip lock on her, for the victory kiss.

The security people just went berserk. They frowned on Bobby, a dirty, grimy race car driver just getting out of the car after a dirt track race and grabbing their Sabrina like that.

I presume the British people are not quite as conservative today as they were then in 1955, at least according to what we see on television.

We had one more surprise in store that first evening.

We were all quite dirty after that race, so one of the officials asked if we would like to take a quick bath. We quickly agreed, with thanks.

Herringway Stadium was a beautiful place where they had many indoor and outdoor sports, including ice hockey and motorcycle racing. There were several buildings on the grounds.

A couple of officials went off to prepare for the baths and others escorted us to the building where it was to happen.

We went running in expecting to find some showers, but there was a huge tub, about the size of a Lincoln Town Car, right in the middle of the floor, so big, and filled with water.

We were surprised, but I figured it would be impossible, time wise, for us to take a bath one at a time. It had to be meant to be a community deal. Ah, these surprising Brits.

I got my clothes off real quick and got in there and washed my face and head in a hurry before the other guys got in there.

It was really good and we enjoyed it and had a real laugh about it.

We had one more shocker ahead for the next day.

I have told you about all the promotion and hype for that first race, and that the seven of us were partners with Digger Pugh, Vanadore and Davenport, to a degree.

There were 43,000 people who paid admission to get in that night. It was unbelievable to us, that many people attending a race on what was essentially a long third of a mile oval dirt track. You can bet there were smiles on our faces.

The agreement was that we would be paid the regular purse money for this first of a series of races, plus some promotion money which had been co-promoted by the American promoters and the Englishman.

Digger Pugh had hoped that featuring the American drivers' invasion against the home country drivers would excite the public more than any other race that had been held there. Vanadore and Davenport were sure that would happen and we, the drivers, agreed.

The deal was struck that we would receive a percentage of the gate for whatever customers we drew over their previous record attendance.

We did deliver that night!

The next day, Vanadore and Davenport went in to see Digger Pugh and I was chosen to be the spokesman for the drivers.

Digger Pugh responded to their request for the money, "Look here, do you have that in writing?" Of course, they didn't, but we all knew that we had all agreed on this.

Pugh said, "I'm sorry boys, but that's all there is to it. Here's what you have coming."

We had to take the money he offered, the regular purse. He wouldn't budge. He was always surrounded by men who appeared to be his goon squad, and he did have power there.

Pugh had cheated us - stolen is the word - $4,800. Big money in those days.

Vanadore and Davenport did file suit on our behalf and we did have to go to court a few times, but nothing came of it.

All the time, we were continuing to race for the man and were seeing him a couple of times every week. He was not embarrassed, but it aggravated us. Particularly me, as I had been the spokesman, I felt somewhat responsible to the other six. This certainly gave me a foul taste in my mouth concerning Mr. Digger Pugh, and this led to my later meeting with the gentlemen from Scotland Yard.

Well, we had our world championship race and the welcome to England behind us so we went on to the other races which had been scheduled for our six months' tour.

As mentioned, the first race was scored on a team basis, but from here on out, the scoring and payoff were more conventional, every driver for himself, whether Yank or Brit. Every man would be trying to win the race for himself.

I had the good luck and pleasure of winning the race at

Liverpool, then another race back at Herringway Stadium, one at Eastborne and at Plymouth. We had a good time. All of us seven from the red, white and blue had our shares of good finishes and the English lads did, also. It was good racing.

We raced every Saturday night, sometimes twice a week and we did not necessarily all seven of us race at the same track those mid-week nights.

There might be two or three tracks operating at the same time in various parts of England, and all the promoters wanted to have the Yanks as the big attraction, so we would split up.

Vanadore had arranged for us to use a large London garage in the Wood Green section of London to work on our race cars, and we all lived in residential boarding houses and hotels in London, usually all at the same hotel. Each of the seven terrors paid his own living expenses from the weekly salary ($100 for me and my car, $50 each for the others) and the money each of us could earn at each night's race. We shared rooms to save expenses.

There were times we would change hotels, just for a change of scenery. Once, we were invited to leave.

Possum Jones and I were out of town at a race and when we came home we found all our luggage in the lobby and then we had to track down the new location of the rest of the gang. I never did find out why we were evicted.

After we had shut down the British drivers that first night at the Stadium, the word got around the country. The local track operators would telephone Vanadore and Davenport and beg them to sent the Yanks.

Whichever town we wanted to visit and whichever gave Vanadore the best deal, that's where we would race. Vanadore and Davenport would keep that deal money and we would keep the prize money each of us earned. I presume that Digger Pugh was also getting a piece of the Vanadore deal money. Lester and Buddy never told me. In fact, I never asked.

On the other hand, promoters would frequently call me or one of the other drivers at the garage and ask us to influence Vanadore to send us to his track. Often a promoter would hand me or others $100 or $200 each, depending on the circumstances.

Deal money was a way of life there, just as it was back home in that era. Today, everything is big business on the major circuits.

* * *

Then, we went to a race at Southampton and we were exposed to a new stock car racing gimmick, one I hope to never see again.

The driver who caused the most excitement each night - that's their word, "excitement" - would get ten pounds extra money on top of what he won normally. This was paid no matter what he did that caused the excitement, good or bad. Can you imagine?

The economy in England was not that great in those days. Gasoline at home was selling for 19 cents a gallon, 50 cents a gallon there. Ten pounds was said to be about the equivalent of a week's pay for the average gas station attendant or mechanic.

The extra award encouraged mayhem sometimes rather than good racing. We would be careful, try to zip by them as quickly as we could, being cautious all the time when the bonus bounty was in effect.

One day, a British driver came by our shop and wanted to work on his car, a '37 Ford sedan, the old stagecoach as they called it.

He was packing old clothes and papers in the back of the car and he explained he was going after the ten pounds bonus. He said he was going to saturate the clothes and paper with gasoline. He had rigged a detonator up front.

He was going to drive the car into a corner, turn it over and detonate it, blow up the gasoline fumes and let the car burn.

The race was at Herringway Stadium and all of us watched that guy very carefully, because we did not want to be near when he flipped the car.

He did do it and he did collect the ten pounds.

With that background, we journeyed to Southampton and my own fateful confrontation.

One of the British cars crossed in front of me and I had no place to go. Not uncommon at all in short track racing. I spun my car and tapped his ever so slightly.

Suddenly, I can imagine my eyes were wide, wide open,

because here came this joker straight at my car. He had on big heavy bumpers and he was headed straight for me, head on.

It was obviously going to be one heck of a wreck.

I popped the gear shift into reverse, braced myself and tried to back up a little to lessen the blow. It did help some.

Wham! Bam! The blow almost knocked the chassis of my car out from under the engine. The engine and transmission all just moved forward.

That crash did a lot of damage to my race car, even more than I realized when I quickly examined the situation after shaking off the momentary grogginess.

The water pumps, which also served as the engine supports, broke and the engine dropped down onto the cross member.

The oil pan was bent and shoved against the crankshaft inside the engine.

As the crankshaft was turning, it cut an ugly groove in the oil pan and also cut into the cross member. The stress cracked the crankshaft.

We never expected that much damage and didn't realize the crankshaft was ruined until quite some time later, which I will explain.

Even without realizing the crankshaft damage, the crash put my car out of the race.

Bobby Myers and I went back to London to work on my car.

We had previously made arrangements with the operator of a gas station that had a junkyard so we could pick up all kinds of Ford parts there.

First, I thought the trouble was mostly with the oil pan being bent out of shape. We bought a pan from the used parts man and checked out the engine supports. Then I bought two water pumps and we put them on, so the car would have engine supports.

We checked out everything, we thought, put everything into place, including a new radiator and other parts.

Everything looked fine until I climbed into the race car and hit the starter. That old thing just said, "KLUNKK!"

We had not looked into the engine. Never even thought that the crash would do that much damage.

Then I noticed the marks on the cross member and

realized, "Oh, my God! It broke the crankshaft!"

I had been running the 3⅜ bore over a 4⅛ inch stroked crankshaft and about the closest place to get a stroked crank was Honest Charley Card's Speed Shop in Chatanooga, Tenn.

There I was with a modified flat head Ford race car in England and all my spare parts gone. I didn't have any good stuff to put back into it, certainly not a racing crankshaft.

Digger Pugh, after he had clipped us out of that $4,800 for the first race, had been wanting to buy my race car and separate Bobby Myers and me from the other American drivers. Bobby was driving a car provided by Vanadore and Davenport and I was driving my own race car so I could do just about what I wanted, choose the tracks I wanted to race, and Digger didn't really like that.

Remember, I had said that I would not forget what Pugh had done, cheating us out of the bonus money promised for the first race's capacity crowd. I knew it wouldn't do any good to get mad, especially over there in his country. But sometimes there might be an opportunity to get even.

So, regardless of my low opinion of the man, we all had to work with him during our stay. Pugh had talked a few times about wanting to buy my race car and I had listened politely, but made no commitment, nor did I flatly refuse.

So, here I was with a race car with an engine that would not run and no way of getting it repaired with my limited resources there. It would have been different in South Carolina. I would probably have had a new crankshaft within a day or two.

I was finished. My tour of England was about to come to an abrupt halt as suddenly as if I had hit the outside wall at Darlington head on!

What to do? The wheels began to turn up there in my head. I told Bobby Myers what I was thinking and he acknowledged for the first time that he wanted to go home. He was homesick, a good ole country boy, and he would gladly trade the fish and chips for some North Carolina grits and gravy.

I telephoned Digger Pugh and told him that I was ready to sell the race car, told him where we were and that both Bobby and I were ready to quit the American promoters and would go racing for him.

He said, okay, he would be at the gas station and auto parts yard shortly.

We had bolted everything back on the race car and there was no damage visible. I wanted to be sure that he could not attempt to start the car. Obviously, that is the first thing a customer would do.

A man was riding a bicycle past the gas station, so I called him over, took out the auto battery and sat it in the basket on the bicycle, told the man to keep it and bid him goodbye. He said his thanks and rode away, happy to have a perfectly good automobile battery as a gift. He couldn't figure out why, but he was happy. He probably muttered something like, "Crazy Americans," as he pedaled down the road.

We spent the remainder of the time shining the race car. This was to be a classic sting such as you have seen on television where the guys in the white hats lower the boom on the one in the black hat . . . getting even!

Digger arrived, followed by one of his trucks and a driver, planning to truck the race car directly to Plymouth where Bobby or I would race for him the following night.

Of course, Digger wanted to start the car, but I told him the battery had been damaged in that crash at Southampton and he would have to get a new one.

Our deal was that Digger would pay me $3,500 cash and Bobby and I would split the driving. I would take it one race, Bobby the next.

Digger was exploring all the angles. He had been promoting some of the tracks that we raced on and he also owned some of the cars which raced, just as Vanadore and Davenport owned six cars.

He figured that with owning my good car and Bobby and me driving for him, that would improve his chances of winning more races and more money. He didn't like to see Vanadore taking the money out of his, Digger's, purses.

While waiting for Pugh to arrive at the gas station, Bobby and I had also been busy. After some phone calls, we learned that we could catch a ship leaving Liverpool for New York.

Bobby and I and Pugh's driver pushed the race car up onto his trailer, then Bobby and I rode to Digger's house to be paid. The house, the gas station, the team garage and even the subway were all fairly close to one another.

As he counted out the money, I had no qualms, suffered no conscience pangs. He had shown himself to be greedy, scheming and a cheater. This was not a ripoff, just equalizing things a bit.

Besides, he got something for his money. The car, even without a crankshaft, was worth at least $1,000. That was more than he gave us at the Stadium race.

Digger wanted me to ride to Plymouth with him in his Jaguar. I said, "No, I can't split with Bobby like that. He'd have to ride the train, so we'll both ride the train and we'll meet you in Plymouth tomorrow."

He reluctantly said, "Okay," but I could see that my refusal bothered him, although he wasn't sure why.

Bobby and I left the house and walked the short distance to the subway, headed for the railroad station and the train which would carry us to Liverpool.

Remembering the puzzled look of Digger, I commented to Bobby, "You know, he's just sharp enough that if he smells a rat or something, with all his connections he might just call down to that train station to check whether two Yanks had bought tickets to Plymouth.

"We'd better get off this subway and go buy two tickets to Plymouth and just throw them away. It will cost a little money, but that's better than being bruised. Then we will get back on the subway and go to the other station and take the train to Liverpool."

We did that, walked into the train station to get the tickets to Plymouth and, would you believe, there sat that turkey. He had driven over there and waited to see if we had intended to go to Plymouth.

There is a cliche, "It takes a crook to know a crook." While I didn't and still don't consider that I was a crook, it surely proved to me that when a man is as devious as was Digger Pugh, he's way ahead of an honest man who temporarily attempts to be devious for some good reason.

Of course, when he saw us, he figured everything was all right.

But, Digger stayed around and talked and talked. I guess he had time on his hands. I don't think he was checking on us any more. For whatever reason, he did hang around and soon here came the damn Plymouth-bound train, southbound, and we needed to go north, desperately. We were fast running out of time, we thought. We did have a schedule to keep. We didn't know it then, but that schedule was not going to matter at all.

We also wanted to get away from Pugh, get out from under before his mechanics telephoned him from Plymouth to advise that he had purchased a race car with a blown engine.

There was no choice but to get on the southbound train. Digger saw us on the train, and into one of the compartments they had on the train. He even shut the door to the compartment after we went in and got off the train just as it was ready to leave.

Perhaps he was still suspicious. Regardless, we were on a train headed in the wrong direction.

Bobby asked, "Now, what the hell are we going to do?"

I figured, "The engineer is going to have to stop this train somewhere before we get to Plymouth."

He did, about 19 miles south of London at the Reading station. We hauled off that train, went running around and bought tickets right back to London.

We had to go back through that same train station and we were afraid Digger might still be hanging around talking to someone else. But, we had to take the chance. Fortunately, he was nowhere in sight.

We had to dodge him because he had a reputation for having things done to people he didn't like.

From the train station, we boarded the subway and went over to the other London railroad station, bought our tickets and headed north.

They did have an express train to Liverpool in the morning, but we didn't dare hang around all night.

With all his connections, Digger could get on the telephone and locate two Yanks hanging around the railroad station. It was a touchy situation and we knew it.

We knew that as soon as his driver got the race car to Plymouth, they would put in a battery and try to back it off the trailer. Then they would phone Digger Pugh.

We rode the local trains all night, criss-crossing the area.

Now we are dockside at the Britannia and in line to go through Customs. The Britannia was nice looking, very inviting.

When my turn came and I called out my name, the Customs man said, "Mr. Crider, Mr. Myers, there is a man from Scotland Yard over there who wants to talk to you."

At first, I expected that Pugh had called the police to say that we had stolen some jewelry or something out of his house, or some other trumped up charge.

But the man from the Yard did not tell us about any specific charge.

He said, "A man is trying to stop you two from going home."

He let that sink in a little bit, then he said, "I'll tell you what. We know this man a little bit, too. You boys go ahead. He hasn't any case against you. You get on that ship and go home and good luck to you."

Boy, did we feel good. The ship was supposed to pull out at ten o'clock that morning and we would soon be on the high seas, on our way to home, sweet home.

Almost, that is. Almost! Not so fast, fellows!

In some way, Murphy's law became Crider's law: If something can go wrong, it will.

Would you believe they had a dock workers' strike and we sat on that ship for five days and five nights, afraid to even go up on deck.

We really didn't know what to expect, we had heard so many things about Pugh.

I'll tell you, when you are in a jam, your imagination can run wild, really wild.

Finally, we had more than we could stand, so I asked the purser, "Isn't there another ship anywhere that's going to the States?" He said, "Yes sir, the Queen Elizabeth is going to leave from Southampton and if you want to, we have an express train and we will send you right on down there. Your tickets will be good and everything will be fine."

"For God's sake, if you can get us on that express train, we will be so grateful."

The train took us right through London, but it was express, and we got on the Queen Elizabeth and came back to the United States.

It was so good to be home.

There is one humorous postscript.

They didn't have hot dog and hamburger stands as we did. Everything was fish and chips, which was nice enough, but we did tire of them as a steady diet.

At some of the places where we stayed, we told them about hamburgers and a few started buying the supplies and cooking for us, then they found that other customers liked them, so we started something.

After we got off the ship in New York, Bobby and I were walking down the street looking around, because we had time to kill before the bus left for Greensboro, N.C.

As we decided to get something to eat, we looked up and saw a big sign, "Fish and Chips."

"What say, Bobby, shall we go for it?" So our first meal in the States was fish and chips.

We got on back to Greensboro and Billy Myers and others in the family were waiting to take Bobby to Winston-Salem, and I continued on my way to South Carolina.

We both started racing again, back in the Southland.

Vanadore and Davenport and the other five drivers stayed in England another couple months after we left. Lester and Buddy had closed or leased their Carolinas race tracks for the spring.

We had been there from March through June, so our season was just beginning.

After the other fellows came home, we all talked and laughed about my hassle with Digger Pugh.

It seems that Pugh and his men got some parts together and they called over to the States and had a crankshaft shipped to them.

Digger put an English driver in my old car and they did win some races, too.

I never did hear from Pugh, who had a publicity man named Peter Arnold. Although he worked for Pugh, he was a good guy, and didn't like some of the things his boss did. He came to the States and looked me up a few times, until he died a half dozen years ago.

Ardun OHV Conversion for Ford Flathead V-8.

Daytona Beach 200. The Starting Lineup, 1949.

Halfway Point.

The Winner! Marshall Teague in a '39 Ford Sedan.

THE BEST RACE DRIVER
YOU EVER SAW

I guess for most of us there are many twists and turns in each of our lives, but there is usually one particular time or particular place where one's life takes a definite turn, a new direction that turns out later to be very important.

Mine happened in Henderson, N.C., in the early '50s, in fact, 1951.

I had gone to the Henderson Speedway to watch an auto race. No big deal, just a little recreation.

I was standing in the infield watching a guy who was practicing out on the track in his modified Ford. He would run two or three laps and the engine would start skipping.

He brought the car into the pits and he checked the water in the radiator, filled it up with more water and he went back out onto the track.

I noticed that the radiator overflow hose was spitting water on the distributor cap.

When he came in the next time, I was standing behind the wire spectator fence, of course, but I called to him and said, "Look, man, why don't you quit filling that thing with water? It's going to seek its own level anyway. Try it like that."

He did and his car ran really good for quite a while after that, no engine skipping and it didn't run hot.

He thought that was pretty good. I learned later that this was his first race car.

We got to talking and he asked me, before the race started, "You wouldn't happen to be a race car driver, would you?"

I said, "Yeah. Matter of fact I am, about the best you ever saw." Of course, I knew and you know now that I had never run a race car before. I had run many cars on dirt roads, but I had never driven a race car before. I had been to a lot of races and I liked them. That's why I was at Henderson to watch this one.

He asked me, "Why don't you be the driver and I'll be the mechanic, the pit crew."

"Okay, that's fine with me." So it was that in July 1951 at age 20, I became a professional racing driver.

Over the fence I went and everything worked out all right.

In fact, I finished fourth in the race. I'll never forget that day.

After the race, I was so happy and so nervous, trying to get home to Greensboro in a hurry and to tell everybody what had happened, damned if I didn't wreck my own car on the road. I ran up on the back end of another car because I was not paying enough attention.

Anyway, I drove for that fellow for a while and eventually ended up getting my own race car.

Actually, I traded my '39 Chevrolet street car for a race car, a '36 Ford Coupe. Of course that left me without highway transportation.

I would drive the race car to the gas station, which was only about a block away, then wait until some friends or my daddy would come by and convince one of them to hook up my tow bar to their trailer hitch and take me to the race track. My Daddy managed to avoid going near that gas station most weekends.

That is the way auto racing began for me, eventually a rewarding, exciting and adventuresome career.

IMPRESSING THE HOME FOLKS

After racing around the Carolinas for a while, I had the opportunity to run the famous beach and road course at Daytona Beach in 1958.

There are many folks who will tell you today, almost three decades later, that the beach and road course was the scene of the best stock car racing ever run, and those folks include the Daytona Beach natives and transplants, as well as racing fans from many sections of the country.

The cars would run two miles north on the wide, hard-packed sand of the Atlantic Ocean beach, broadslide as they approached the North Turn, roar through the short man-made stretch of crushed shell and sand, on to the two-lane blacktop asphalt of South Atlantic Avenue, then two miles down to the South Turn, another left to the beach, and back up the course.

The track conditions of the beach were whatever Mother Nature had created the night before. A northeast wind would leave a smooth beach, a west wind could leave it with too many wavy bumps. The two short turns across the sand dunes were constructed with the use of bulldozers, road graders and rollers, attempting to pack in the tons of crushed shell which were trucked in from elsewhere in Volusia County.

No matter how hard the turns were packed before the race, the race cars would dig them up after a few laps and that made for some exciting racing, thrilling drivers and spectators alike.

Many of my relatives were going down to Daytona Beach to watch me compete in the big time, and I was proud.

I told the relatives that they should go down to the grandstands on the outside of the South Turn, where they would see the cars roar off the asphalt road, dig their way through the soft dirt of the turn, then swing onto the beach and head north.

I told them, "That's where most of the action is." I was to drive a Sportsman car in the Saturday race. Really, that was the place to be. Some cars would fail to negotiate the turn and would go off the outside banking. The grandstand was set far enough back so the cars would not endanger spectators. Some cars would go over the outside bank beyond the end of the stands and slide across the beach and into the edge of the ocean water.

The thrills were not as abundant at the North Turn, because if a driver saw he had miscalculated, he could use the escape road straight up the beach, make a U-turn and come back to the North Turn and resume the race. Approaching the South Turn left no alternative. The driver would either make it through the turn or over it, and over it would be over and out.

I knew the folks would get their thrills there and I also determined that I would show them my skills. No one would outdo me in the South Turn as long as my homefolks were watching.

I remember the details of that race well. I was driving that day for Joe Johnson of Charleston, S.C.

There was one hair-raising experience that day. Paul Goldsmith was driving a 1950 Olds modified, sponsored by the Air Lift people. Paul and I roared down the narrow backstretch road side by side. He was on the inside.

We reached that spot, a small hump in the blacktop, and neither of us backed off, not even a little bit. Being on the outside, I was the one who was in trouble, and Paul knew that.

What he didn't know was that I could not bring myself to back off because I knew all those friends and relatives were watching for me.

Finally, Goldsmith showed a little more sense than did I and he backed off. I let my car go deeper into the corner and turned hard left, with the car in a power broadslide, right in front of the Olds.

As we roared through the turn, my old Ford was right up on the outside edge of the track, as high up on the banked turn as possible, the old wheels spinning and digging. The car was trying to stay up on that banking and it made it! To this day, I have never figured how I could have been so lucky.

Up the beach we went and I was way ahead of Paul. He just backed off completely when he saw what a fool thing I had done, I guess.

Every lap, when I got to the North Turn, I took it easy to be sure I would finish the race, but I always showed off a bit in the South Turn, but not quite as bad as that first lap.

There is a punch line, a kicker to that little tale, but first let me describe the situation for you racing fans who never did see the great racing on the beach.

Traffic and parking were always a problem for that famous 4.1-mile race course, about 20 miles south of Daytona Beach.

There were wooden grandstands across the outside of both the North and South turns, but hundreds of racing fans lined the sand dunes along that two miles of beach, what would be the infield on a normal oval race track.

The high tide area of the beach was reserved for about a half-mile north of the South Turn for the pit area for the race crews and their equipment. Spectator auto parking was permitted for the remaining mile or so between the turns, but even with the cars in two or three rows, fender to fender, the space would not accommodate all who wanted to be in there.

Thousands of autos were parked on the beach north of the North Turn, literally about a four-mile-long parking lot, three or four or five cars deep.

Because of the long walk for the later arrivals, Ford Motor Co. men came up with one of their "better ideas" and provided free bus transportation from the parked cars to the North Turn grandstand. You can be sure that the General Motors and Chrysler fans put their rivalries aside and were happy to accept the free rides from Ford.

Incidentally, for those readers who did attend those beach races, the Old Timers Lounge is still operating in the same location. although the grandstand is long gone.

Now for that kicker postscript I promised you.

After the race when I finally made contact with all the friends and relatives, I learned that they had been caught up in the traffic jam and got no further than the North Turn grandstand, where I had so carefully driven every lap.

I don't think they were much impressed with my "stroking" style of driving.

That was the last time I ever tried to tell my folks where to sit at a race track. Nor did I ever try to impress my friends with my driving.

From then on, I drove according to the racing conditions and whatever they saw was what it was, warts and all.

As for the results of that 164-mile Sportsman Modified race, Edwin "Banjo" Matthews was the winner in a 1955 Modified Ford, averaging 97.381 miles per hour.

Paul Goldsmith finished fifth in his Modified Olds and I was 13th in my 1940 Ford Sportsman class car.

The following day, Sunday, Paul Goldsmith was the winner of the 160-mile, 39-lap Grand National race, the final race on the beach and road course. Goldsmith had qualified his 1958 Pontiac on the pole for that race, with a new record of 140.570 mph. The speed of the race was 101.18 mph.

Thus, my friend Goldy earned a unique place in the record books, the only man to win a motorcycle race and to win a stock car race on that great beach and road course. Paul was a national motorcycle racing champion long before he ever drove a stock car or an Indianapolis car.

SPEED ON SAND

$\mathbf{T}$he world of stock car racing owes so much to "The World's Most Famous Beach" just for being there when it was needed.

As William R. Tuthill wrote in his book *Speed On Sand,* "It was the speed exploits in Ormond Beach that finally gripped the imagination of the early day inventors (of the automobile) and paved the way for today's giant automobile industry."

Right after the turn of the century, some automotive pioneers were sitting the porch of the Ormond Hotel (which at the time of this writing is still standing) and they discussed the various new automobiles and their strong and weak points.

Someone suggested a race on the beach. Alexander Winton had already built and raced his Winton Bullet and he agreed to bring the car to Florida for a race.

Ransom E. Olds, then manufacturing automobiles, agreed to build a race car and bring it to Florida.

Early in 1902, Ransom Olds and his Pirate, Winton and his Bullet, lined their cars side by side on the beach, determined to each prove that his car was the better.

The result, both cars ran identical speeds, 57 mph.

Later that spring, William J. Morgan of Newark, N.J., a magazine writer, saw a newspaper photograph of an automobile on the beach. He approached the owners of the Ormond Hotel and soon a racing tournament was scheduled in 1903. The rest is well documented in the automotive history archives.

For stock car racing, the next important happening was the arrival in Daytona Beach of William Henry Getty France, Anne France and their son, William C. France.

They were enroute from Washington, D.C., to a new life in the Miami area, but they stopped in Daytona Beach and never did get to Miami until years later, and then only for a visit.

After Sir Malcolm Campbell had taken his world land speed record car to try out the Bonneville, Utah, Salt Flats, someone came up with an idea to keep racing alive in the Daytona Beach area, a 250-mile race on the beach March 8, 1936.

Milt Marion was the winner in a Ford V8 and Big Bill France finished fifth in a Ford V8. Later, France took over the promotion of the stock car races on the beach, and NASCAR was organized in Daytona Beach after World War II.

As Houston A. Lawing once wrote, "If you want to race, Daytona's the place!"

Traditionally, the Flagler and Volusia counties area including Ormond Beach and Daytona Beach between the Atlantic Ocean and the Intracoastal Waterway has been called the Peninsula.

Actually it is an island, two to three miles wide and about 50 miles long between the Matanzas Inlet north of Marineland and the Ponce Inlet, just south of the once famed South Turn.

It is not being overly dramatic to recall that this island, and its World's Most Famous Beach, made many contributions to the growth of the American automotive industry and professional auto racing, partly by chance and partly because of its availability and the physical qualities provided so amply by Mother Nature.

A FARMER WHO BECAME A RACER

While you are reading about the escapades, exploits, adventures, troubles and happiness of my racing friends and me, you may be wondering, "Exactly who is this guy Curtis 'Crawfish' Crider? What is he all about? Where is he coming from? Can I believe what he is telling me? Should I like him or not?"

Everyone wants to be liked by his friends and athletes want to be liked by their fans.

You will be making those judgments as you read these pages.

I am most concerned that you will like the friends about whom I have written. That's the purpose of this book.

As a racing driver I did not win 200 Grand National/Winston Cup races as did Richard Petty, nor millions of dollars, nor a Grand National Championship, but I did finish second in that world championship stock car race in England.

My auto racing career has been great because I have had the pleasure of meeting and sometimes competing against some really wonderful people.

If you are looking for gossip or criticism about the folks I have known for four decades, you won't find it here.

I was born October 7, 1930, a Tuesday, in Danville, Va., below the Mason-Dixon Line, a native Southerner and proud of it. Let's use the well worn phrase once - and not again in this book - a "good ole boy."

Actually, folks have used that expression to describe

Southerners for years, a term of friendship.

Ever since the big city sports writers and broadcasters in the Northeast and Midwest discovered major league NASCAR stock car racing, the expression has been used to identify all stock car racers, and not necessarily as a compliment.

My ancestry is Dutch-German. My father, Wade Crider, my brother Ike and sister Faye, Mrs. Iva Perdue, now live in Greensboro, N.C.

My mother, Musie "Mama Boots" Crider, is deceased.

On the personal side, my lovely wife Louise and our son Curtis Dean Crider, age nine in February 1987, live in Ormond Beach, Florida. There are two grown children, Garrison Wade "Chip" Crider and Jan, who is married to race driver Mark Gibson. Louise and I were married in 1977.

My first wife, Mary Frances Wilson Crider, and I were divorced in 1974. She lives in the Daytona Beach area and would you believe we are all good friends and visit together often, Mary Frances, Louise, our three children and me.

I was raised in a farm family. My father grew tobacco.

There came a day during my sixteenth year when I decided that I had had enough of farming.

I was working in the middle of a field on the farm in Chapel Hill, N.C., when I decided to retire. I wrapped the reins around the plow and walked away from the plow and the mule.

Daddy asked, "Where are you going?"

"I'm leaving! I figure the next time I tell a mule to get up, that mule is going to be sitting in my lap."

Regardless, I went on home. Dad didn't think very much of that idea and both he and Mama were upset and raised a lot of sand about it.

I was almost 16, so I just got my clothes together and went to my uncle, who had a gasoline service station in Schoolfield, near Danville, Va.

Daddy had always been a mechanic for the people of our local area and I had helped him since I was ten years old, taking apart cars and making some repairs. By the time I was almost 16, I was a pretty good mechanic.

I stayed and worked with my uncle for a couple of years. I had dropped out of high school at the end of the tenth grade. But after working for my uncle, I joined the U.S. Air Force, and finished high school while in that service.

From 1948, for the next few years, I travelled a lot, worked on radar assignments mostly, went to Cheyenne, Wyoming, for heavy equipment school and served in Japan. Went to a couple of schools there, so I was learning trades and getting an education at the same time.

After returning home from service with the Air Force, I began attending short track stock car races as a spectator, and I have told you about the chance encounter which led to my becoming a professional stock car racing driver.

As you know, racing in those days was on the short tracks, mostly dirt surface.

The everyday drivers of those post-war years have become legends since and their names and accomplishments will live forever in the record books.

Buddy Shuman, Cotton Owens, Speedy Thompson, Fireball Roberts, Buck Baker, Gober Sosebee, Nero Steptoe, the fabulous flock of Flocks, Carl the champion rifle marksman, Bob and Fonty and later Tim Flock, the star race drivers, and let's not forget the ladies of the era, Ethel Flock Mobley, Louise Smith and Sara Christian. The list can go on and on, Red Byron, Marshall Teague, Herb Thomas, Little Joe Weatherly, Joe Lee Johnson and Bobby Johns. Along with Bobby Myers was his brother Billy Myers, and the fellow from Virginia, North Carolina and South Carolina, Crawfish Crider.

In my single days, footloose and carefree, I lived wherever somebody had a race car for me to drive. If the man for whom I was driving lived in Charleston, I lived in Charleston. If I switched rides, I might live in Colombia, Florence, Abbeville or Greenwood. You name it, I have probably lived there.

In fact, when I came through the gate towing my race car one day, the track announcer said, "Here comes Crawfish Crider from somewhere in South Carolina." My reputation as a gypsy was well-founded.

I have been involved in stock car racing for 35 years, as a driver, car builder, mechanic, promoter, official and public address announcer. My daughter Jan is married to race driver Mark Gibson, a track champion, and my son Garrison Wade "Chip" Crider is doing real well with his brake and muffler shop in Abbeville, S.C., where he was born. As they say, the beat goes on.

I have raced Modifieds, Sportsman cars and Grand Nationals and I have won track championships and state championships. I am a member of the Pure Oil (now Unocal 76) Darlington Record Club, 1961, qualifying a Mercury at 119.250 mph, a record at that time.

Of all my auto racing experiences, I have most enjoyed meeting people and having long lasting friendships.

Perhaps I am an eternal optimist, as one friend said, but I do see the good in people and more or less ignore the bad.

Certainly there are some jerks in this world, but those I forget about.

The memories that last are about the good folks, and they are the big majority.

Even that British fellow I wrote about earlier, Mr. Digger Pugh, had some good qualities. He made it possible for us to tour England for several months, and that fostered some friendships that have lasted 30 years.

For that I thank Mr. Digger Pugh.

I have a motto, one which I borrowed from Elzie Wylie "Buck" Baker Sr.: "Give out, but don't give up."

FURTHER SOUTH IN DIXIE

After living in North Carolina for a while, I decided it was time to move on, to South Carolina, but even that move proved to give me a problem.

I had been having a rough time with the police in North Carolina. It seemed that I could not move on the highway without receiving a speeding ticket. Some I deserved, but other tickets I felt were unreasonable.

I had also heard there were good races in South Carolina.

I hooked up my old race car and put my clothing and stuff in the back of the tow car and was headed out of there, southward bound.

I didn't get 30 miles out of Greensboro, N.C., before I was pulled over and ticketed for towing too slow.

The policeman saw all the stuff in the back of the tow car, boxes of clothes and tools and even the race car was loaded with spare parts.

He asked me, "Where are you going?"

I knew that if I told him that I was going to South Carolina he would have made me pay up for the ticket right there and then.

"We're moving down here on the Burlington Road and thank goodness this is the last load."

So he gave me the ticket and I went on my way.

The next stop was Columbia, S.C.

Those were good ole days. They were fun.

Among the local drivers around there in those days were Head Hamby, Johnny Deavers, Billy Franklin and Jimmy

Roland. The racing was really good around Columbia.

I made friends with M.C. Smelgroves and the folks at Smelgroves' garage, and the folks at Standard Auto Parts who agreed to sponsor me and give me some parts and some help. I kept the car at Smelgroves.' We all became good, fast friends.

Sooner or later I found the town of Greenwood, S.C., and the Greenwood Fairgrounds Speedway.

I raced there quite a bit, did well and began to make a name for myself with the fans. Well, most of them. I'll tell you about one of the fans next.

Darlington Raceway Action, Early '50s.

MARRIAGE SLIGHTLY CURBS THE GYPSY LIFESTYLE

One race day at Greenwood, S.C., a situation occurred which turned my life around, all for the better.

The Fairgrounds Speedway was built around a football field, with the typical stadium setup, two end zones, grandstands on both sides of the playing field (and race track, too).

The rest rooms were in the end zone just outside the racing oval, but so were the pits. The fans would have to come down out of the grandstands and walk through the pit area to the rest rooms. It was no great problem, just a bit different from the setup at most race tracks of that day.

As I worked on my race car a short time before the race, one of my guys said. "Look over there."

There was a fine lady headed for the ladies' room.

"I just have to meet that lady," I told my crew members, put down my tools, wiped my hands and walked over to the rest room building and waited.

When the lady came out, I politely introduced myself, "I'm Curtis 'Crawfish' Crider. What's your name?"

She looked at me sort of funny and I could see that the name Crawfish Crider meant very little. I was a little surprised. In fact, dismayed.

She replied, "I'm Mary Frances Wilson."

I said, "I have to go to work right now, but maybe I will see you later on, if it is okay." She told me where she and her friends were sitting in the grandstand.

After the race, I quickly went to the grandstand as she and her friends were fixing to leave, and we talked a bit more.

Ours was not one of those great story book romances about which movies are made, but we did date a lot and went to a lot of races where I competed and she watched.

We enjoyed each other and one day, enroute to a race, I proposed and gave her the traditional ring.

Mary Frances accepted, but she warned, "We met at a race track, we have gone to a lot of races and you gave me the ring at a race track, but I'll tell you right now, we are not going to be married at a race track!"

We were married, quite properly, in 1954 and we moved in with her parents in Abbeville. Her dad had an auto repair garage right there at the house, so it was quite convenient to keep the race car and work on it there.

When the invitation was received to make the trip to England, we had to make a family decision. Our son Chip was only two months old, but it appeared there might be some money to be earned and Mary Frances and Chip would continue to live with her parents.

Mary Frances realized that it would be an interesting adventure for me, so she readily agreed I should go. It was part of the racing life we had both chosen and this was definitely a chance for me to do something that few people have the opportunity to do.

We had 20 years of happiness together, and two great children. Mary Frances liked to go to races. In fact, even today, she helps score races at the New Smyrna Beach, Florida., Speedway.

Our life styles differed quite a bit. I went to church some, but she went to church more often. Friday and Saturday nights, I liked to go out and shoot pool and drink beer. Mary Frances did not want to do that, and I guess it sort of drove us apart.

We had been through a lot together, good times and not so good ones. Mary Frances had been very sick a while back (more on that later), but she was in good health as we sat on the porch of our house in 1974. We had owned our own home by that time, in Ormond Beach, Florida.

As we talked, we agreed the time had come to do something

about the difference in life styles and we agreed on a friendly divorce.

Because I had my shop there at home, it was agreed that I would keep the house and the shop and Mary Frances would keep what she wanted. Basically, I kept the real estate in Florida and she kept the real estate and property in South Carolina.

So, we were divorced in 1974 and, as mentioned before, we are still friends.

In 1977, after three years of being single again and doing a lot of running around, I began thinking it was time to settle down once more.

I was living in Florida, but there was a young woman in Greensboro, N.C., whom I had known for some time. We had met at a race when mutual friends introduced us.

When I decided that I was tired of the single life, I walked into the house, telephoned my friend in Greensboro, and asked, "Would you like to get married?"

She replied, "To who?"

"Me." And she replied, "Sure."

It was a couple months later before I had time to drive to Greensboro and Louise and her folks had the wedding plans all ready. That was 1977.

Our son, Curtis Dean Crider, is now eight years old. I kidded my son Chip and daughter Jan that they were not moving fast enough to provide me with grandchildren so I had to do something about it myself.

I had been in the asphalt paving business in Ormond Beach, Florida, on U.S. 1, for some time. Along about 1982-1983, a friend bought half interest in the business. We always got along fine, still do.

But, at the end of 1983, I told my friend and partner that I had had enough of that line of work and he readily agreed to split the business even.

I wrote two lists of all the equipment, as evenly valued as possible, and he could choose which list he wanted to keep.

So, we dissolved the partnership in February 1984, right along the time for Daytona Beach Speed Weeks when all my old friends like Junior Johnson and Buddy Baker come to town and get together.

Later I sold the property I owned on U.S. 1, north of Ormond Beach.

Since then, I think I have been busier than when I was working full time. I handled the flagging chores at the Volusia County Speedway and have continuously repaired trucks and bulldozers and road machinery for friends, not only in the Daytona Beach area, but in the Carolinas as well.

You know, when a contractor's equipment breaks, it is very costly to leave it idle. A fellow can't always get factory or dealership service in a hurry, so if I'm available, I'm glad to help old friends.

After all, friends have helped me many times in the past four decades.

While we are thinking about friendship, there are several I want to thank publicly for their help and assistance through the years, for being there and responding when they were asked:

My special thanks go out to P.H. Livingston, Lou Hudson, Jim Scott, Fuzzy Baldini, Bobby Schuyler, Larry Lancaster, David Kay, L.G. Davis, Marty Weeks, Warren Prout, Al Wall, Iva Perdue, Harold Prince, Bill, Buddy and Wayne Reed, Phil McCauley, Jack Wesley, Clarence Sells, Eddie Orr, Lois Wilson, Wimpy Batton, Rene Charland, Horace Tate and that ace photographer from Daytona Beach, Sam Satterwhite, who travelled with me to so many races in the years gone past.

And, while on the subject of people, I have been fascinated with nicknames, some a trifle weird, but all applied to old friends.

Folks such as Doc Collins, Pappa Johns (father of Bobby Johns), Pop Eargle, Whitey Norman, Reb Wickersham, Cotton Lake, Cotton Ownes, Fireball Roberts, Smokey Yunick, Ozark Ike Williams, Marion "The Preacher" Cox, Cricket Dean, Punkin' Dean, my own Mama Boots Crider, Clarence "Tad Pole" Crider, Louise "Hanner" Dean, Fuzzy Baldini, Grasshopper Wilson, Batman Whitaker, Forrest "The Kid" Galahan, Possum Jones, Black Jack DuBruil, Wild Bill Jones, Cantaloupe (Tiny Lund's Mechanic) McKillop, Stick Elliott, Turkey Minton, Jimmy "Nice Guy" Pardue, and Wimpy Batton, Runt Harris, Pee Wee Kirkman, Little Roy Terry and "Daddy Rabbit" Millard.

CURTIS BECOMES A CRAWFISH

Nicknames usually begin quite casually, when someone will make a remark in jest, on the spur of the moment, but often those nicknames stick with a person and often obscure his real first name.

For example, Fireball Roberts. The nickname came because he had a great fast ball as a high school baseball pitcher. How many even know today that his name was Glenn. My friend Junior Johnson. His given name, Robert Glenn Johnson, Jr. The nickname origin is obvious, but did you ever hear anyone call him Robert or Bob?

And then there is Curtis "Crawfish" Crider.

Many years after having moved to Greensboro, N.C., I went back to my birthplace, Danville, Va., to race. In my young, single days.

Enroute to Danville, I met a fine little girl working in a truck stop. She was to be working until midnight. We made a date that I would stop there after the race.

Because we travelled light, with no extra changes of clothing, it was agreed that I would try and stay clean. The guys on the crew would do all the tire changing and other work, and I would drive. A fellow wouldn't get very dirty that way, would he?

You have heard of Murphy's Law, if something can go wrong, it will. Well, Murphy's Law became Crider's Law that night.

During the race, I crossed up the car on the backstretch and up and over I went, outside the track and into a little old creek. Not very deep, but wet and muddy.

The car wasn't damaged and I wasn't hurt, but I guess I looked pretty awful and pretty funny climbing out of the stream and up the bank.

When I got to the pit area, the guys started picking at me and one of them said that I looked like a crawfish, all muddy and wet, coming out of the creek.

From then on, I was Crawfish Crider and many folks never even knew my name was Curtis.

Later, while driving Grand National cars and having need to talk business with automotive executives in Detroit, I felt it would be ridiculous to telephone Detroit and say, "Hey, look here, this is Crawfish Crider."

I figured it would sound much better to say, "Good morning, this is Curtis W. Crider."

Not only were some folks surprised to learn my given name, but others who met Crawfish Crider the first time would say, "My goodness. I pictured you to be a heavy set person."

Guess they figured anyone with that nickname had short legs and waddled.

TINY, SOAPY AND POSSUM

Quite often, nicknames are just the opposite from the way a person looks.

Case in point, Dwayne "Tiny" Lund, who weighed in at about 280 pounds and stood about six feet, five inches. Every inch and every pound a jolly good fellow.

He was a hard race driver and some writers and some film people publicized him as the Hard Charger.

In the pits or at his fishing camp in Monks Corner, S.C., you couldn't find a nicer, more friendly guy.

The folks around Monks Corner and Charleston still remember big Tiny Lund, who had a heart to match his size.

Neil "Soapy" Castles was several years younger than most of us when he started hanging around the garage and racing parts business of Buddy Shuman and Willie Thompson in Charlotte.

Willie was the engine and car builder, Buddy a top driver in those Modified and Sportsman days.

Shuman and Thompson put Castles to work cleaning up the shop, the grease and oil on the floor, parts and tools to be cleaned, engines to be steam cleaned.

They worked Castles so hard that he hardly had time to clean up. He was greasy from head to foot. That's when he was nicknamed Soapy, because he needed some of it. In later years, most folks thought it was a play on the old phrase about blowing soap bubbles, soap castles in the air.

Seriously, there are advantages to a fellow breaking into the mechanical business that way.

By cleaning parts and tools, stocking parts bins and the like, a fellow learns quickly the nomenclature. When the boss tells you to clean a certain set of cylinder heads, you quickly learn to differentiate between the various styles and sizes of cylinder heads, and to which engines they belong.

Soapy Castles learned his trade and became a good race driver, had his own Grand National team, and did quite a lot of stunt driving for movie crews who were making theatrical movies about auto racing years ago.

Castles was one of the seven drivers who made the England series of races in 1955, always ready to help a fellow competitor, one of my good friends through the years and today.

Out of Tampa came Lewis "Possum" Jones.

He was driving for Deese's Garage in Charleston, S.C., and I was racing for Yon Brothers Garage, a short drive down the road.

They were competititors. On the race tracks, Possum and I were competitors, but off the track we were close friends and ran around together, as the phrase goes.

In those days, car owners more or less adopted their young drivers, took them into their homes, each with a room of their own, and the drivers often ate dinner with the families.

When I would go down to Deese's garage about nine or ten in the morning, and ask for Possum, Mr. Deese or his son, Sonny, would say, "He's still in the house."

Sure enough, I'd go in and find him still sacked out.

Whether that's where he got his nickname, I'm not sure, but it surely did fit. That lad liked to sleep more and longer than anyone I have known.

He was one heck of a good race driver.

Possum Jones always drove a race car almost half barefoot, no shoe on his right foot.

I never could stand the hot floor board, but Jones always said he could have a better sense of feeling on the accelerator just wearing a sock, instead of a shoe.

A DRIVING LESSON
FROM A MASTER

Elzie Wylie "Buck" Baker Sr. is one super person, always has been and still is, in my opinion. He was always serious about his racing, yet he was fun, just nice to be around.

During the 1960 Southern 500 at Darlington, S.C., Raceway, I was doing all I could with my old car, going into the corners just as fast as I thought I could possibly make it.

Baker and I came out of the pits one time during a caution period and I was in front of Buck. The field of cars was mostly on the backstretch and the caution period was about to end.

Buck motioned to me to go on. He was obviously anxious to catch up with the tail end of the field, and under NASCAR rules, he could not pass me during a caution period.

I figured I was doing all I could, running wide open because the track was clear between us and the tail end of the pack. I dared not run faster through the corners, especially with my older car.

As we came off the fourth turn, Buck planted the front bumper of his car against my rear bumper, his car pushing mine.

As he carried me into the number one turn, I thought, "Oh, Lord, I'm not going to make it! I just know I ain't going to make it."

Buck backed off his car a bit and that little old Ford of mine settled down in that turn and just sailed through it. It was really beautiful and I couldn't believe it.

Up the backstretch we went and we caught up with the field, well in time to be in line for the green flag resumption of the competition.

Buck Baker went on and won that race.

Buck had taught me something, how to drive through the turns, faster and safely. I picked up two or three positions for myself after he had shown me how to get through the corners. Before that I had been backing off early, not realizing the car's handling capability.

Of course, Buck was not trying to be a teacher, he just wanted to get around faster and I was holding him up. For both of us, regardless of the intent, it worked.

Through the years, Buck Baker and I have had a good relationship, and I was especially happy to see him honored by admission to the National Motorsports Press Association Stock Car Hall of Fame at Darlington. Buck earned that recognition.

From Left: Buck Baker, Jim Reed, Bob Welborn.

RETURNING THE FAVOR

There was a time at the Atlanta International Raceway when Buck Baker was scheduled to drive an Air Lift sponsored Sportsman car on Saturday and his Grand National car Sunday.

Buck had a lot of work back at the shop, then the hurry up drive to Atlanta, so when he qualified the Sportsman car, he was not feeling as well as usual.

His qualifying run put him way back in the starting field, unusual for that car, which was normally good and strong.

Baker had to concentrate on getting his Grand National car ready to go, and as my car was all set, Buck asked, "Curtis, will you go up there and see what is wrong with that Sportsman car. The crew will help you do anything you say. Just go up there, if you will, and check it out, please."

"Okay, Buck."

Baker's crew and I worked on the car, checked it all over. the shocks were good, and so were the springs. We checked the tires and the wedge.

Finally, after some test running, we set the car up exactly as it was when Buck had qualified.

His people and I agreed that we wouldn't tell Buck. We just told him that the car was ready, just perfect, all set to race. Don't worry about a thing.

Sure enough, Buck Baker went out that Saturday and won the Sportsman race in that Air Lift car.

He thanked me for setting up the car for him. We did not want to worry him at the time, by telling him his poor qualifying speed was the fault of his own driving, not the car.

It was a few years later that I leveled with him.

Buck Baker had helped me learn to drive through the turns at Darlington. Now, I had returned the favor, which is what friendship was all about in the formative days of stock car racing.

Buck Baker wins at Darlington, 1953.

GRAND NATIONAL DEBUT AND HUSTLING FOR SPONSORSHIP

After racing around the various dirt tracks in the Sportsman and Modified races, I started to help Cale Yarborough with his Grand National car. I was also working as the service manager at the Ford dealership in Florence, S.C.

I would go to the races with Cale and work on his crew. Some times I would be the only crew member, crew chief or whatever.

One day after a string of bad luck for Cale, he said he wanted to run some of the short tracks around, in between the Grand National events.

I had a nice little '37 Ford already finished, ready to race, so Cale proposed that we trade even, his Grand National car for my Sportsman model.

There I sat with a '58 Grand National car and the Fourth of July Firecracker race coming up at Daytona Beach. I had never driven a Grand National car before, but what the heck.

I worked on the car at the Ford place nights and weekends and finally was ready to leave for Daytona Beach.

By then, I had spent all of our savings just getting the car ready.

I went to the gas station where I regularly traded and asked, "How about filling the tow car with gas, filling the race car with gas and then cash a check for $25 and hold the check until I get back from Daytona?" He agreed.

With the little cash we had at home, the $25 from the gas station, and a full load of gasoline, my wife and two children and I took off for Mecca, Daytona International Speedway.

We still had two or three days after arrival in Daytona Beach before checking in at the Speedway, so I drove around town and found a body shop.

There I told the owner that if he would paint the race car as best he could, in a hurry, I would put his name it. He liked the idea and he did a nice job.

Then I towed the race car around town and stopped at a fast food place called Wattaburger.

I couldn't get both the tow car and race car into his parking lot, so I parked across the street, walked in, found the owner and asked, "How about, would you be interested in putting your name on the side of the race car for the Firecracker 250?"

He said, "Certainly. How much will it be?"

"$150 for the quarter panels."

"That sounds fine. Go ahead and do it."

I went to my Uncle Harry and Aunt Erma Hanks' house in Daytona Beach, put the car in his driveway, got me a brush and some paint and started lettering. I had never done any sign work, so it took me about all day.

I would get almost through with Wattaburger and it would be bigger at one end than it was at the other end, so I'd have to go back and enlarge the letters. I finally got them equalled pretty good.

The next day, I went back to the place, parked across the street and found the boss.

The sign looked pretty good, even better from a distance.

"Yeah, that looks all right. Come into the office."

I had quoted him $150 for the quarter panels, thinking both sides. He said, "Let's see, $150 and $150, that's $300. right?"

"Yes sir, any way you want to figure it."

So he wrote a check for $300. If he thought it was worth $300, I wasn't going to argue. Besides I had not the slightest idea what the going rate for that kind of advertising was. This was all new to me.

We ran the Firecracker race and I earned some money there, so it was not a bad experience. When I returned home, I paid my bills at the neighborhood gas station.

Next came the annual NASCAR Northern Tour, first stop Heidelberg, Pa., just south and west of Pittsburgh.

When we arrived in Heidelberg, a couple days before the race again, I began to look for sponsors. An outboard motor dealer bought the space on the front fenders and I left the Wattaburger name on the quarter panels. The boat dealer was right across the street from the motel.

When Lee Petty arrived, I was out there lettering the signs.

Later, at the track, Petty told some of the fellows, "If you ever see Curtis sitting on a box painting his race car, you might as well unhook because there's sure to be a race around there soon."

The tour took us to races in Toronto and Montreal, Canada.

In those days, we did not have trucks or trailers, just tow bars. Coming back into New York State, there were seven of us towing, fourteen cars in a line, running those winding roads alongside the Hudson River. I was travelling light, with only one crew member, my cousin Jerry Hanks. I was the front driver, leading that parade.

Two girls were signaling for a ride. It was almost sundown, and they were way out in the boondocks in the mountains, soon to be dark, so I stopped to pick them up.

I forgot about the 12 cars behind me and when they all braked quickly it was quite a mess, some of them crossed up across the road.

Thank goodness no car hit another. There was a farmer and his wife sitting on their porch nearby and we about scared them to death, with all the squealing and smoking.

The girls attended a nearby college and they were out hiking and then worried because of the approaching darkness, so decided to try and get a ride.

Then, to make matters worse, we had only gone a half mile when we reached their college.

"Lord, goodness, girls, don't ever do that again. With all that commotion back there and you're only going that short distance, for goodness sakes."

Later, at our destination, Buck Baker said, "Lookahere, Curtis, I know your intentions were good, but the next time something like that happens, how about letting the last car in line pick them up. The first car shouldn't do it, you know."

I couldn't argue with that logic.

Bunkie Blackburn & Friends, Daytona, 1960.

The Crawfish, Daytona, 1960.

WHEELING AND DEALING
WINNING AND LOSING

I have told you about leaving North Carolina. My first race in Columbia, S.C., was a mixture, the good and the bad.

I had a pretty decent little old car, really steady, but there sat Bucky Waters with a brand new No. 14 race car. He was a good builder and had some fast cars and this one was obviously better than my effort.

His regular drivers included Speedy Thompson and Bill Widenhouse. Bucky said he had finished the new car faster than had been expected and he hadn't been able to get in touch with his regular drivers. He did want to try out the new race car, so he had brought it to the Columbia track and had picked up a local driver, Bill Irick, for the shakedown race.

Although a fellow may have been brought up to always be courteous and do right by others, there comes a time when self-preservation and self-advancement requires a bit of maneuvering.

In this business, it doesn't pay to step aside politely when the possibility of a ride in a good car becomes available.

I suggested to Waters, "Bucky, how about letting me drive your new car, and I'll let Irick drive my car?"

"Fine. If you can swing it, it's fine with me."

I approached Irick, "Bill, you're going to drive that No. 14?"

"Yeah. Why?"

"You know how it is. A new car sometimes has bugs in it and stuff like that. For this shakedown run, why don't you drive my car? You know it's pretty steady and I'll try out the

No. 14 for you, if you want me to."

He said, "All right. That's fine with me."

Bill was a good race driver, no two ways about it, but I had convinced Bucky, "You know anything can happen to that car if you let someone else drive it. I have run quite a bit. Somebody else is liable to tear it all to pieces."

That was a prophetic comment, as it turned out.

Bill Irick was in the first heat race with my race car. I watched him for several laps, and all was fine until a couple other cars got out of shape and Irick plowed into them, end over end, every which way. My car was totalled.

We won the feature race that night, with me driving Bucky's new car.

It took me the span of four or five races to get my car repaired.

Bucky's regular drivers were kind enough to let me continue to drive the No. 14 until my car was ready.

"Speedy" Thompson.

A FAMILY AFFAIR

After being a spectator for a few years, my daddy, Wade Crider, decided to get a bit more involved, and my brother Ike caught the racing fever also. They were both good mechanics and Daddy had his own garage.

Instead of building one car for the two of them, they decided to go all the way and build two cars, each his own.

They were racing on the local tracks around Greensboro, with Ike driving his race car and Daddy hiring a driver.

Friends told me that Ike was regularly outrunning Daddy's car and Daddy didn't like that very much.

One day at the garage, Daddy was jumping on his driver, being tired of being outrun, especially by Ike. "Looka here, boy, you just ain't doing it. I know that car will run faster than what you are running around those tracks. Come out here and let me show you."

They rolled Daddy's race car onto the dirt road which ran in front of the garage. There was a 90 degree turn about a quarter mile down the road, plus a 40-acre field.

As Ike and Johnny Handy from Greensboro and others gathered to watch, Daddy took his little old Sportsman car down the road, turned it around and got set. Up the road he raced, past the garage.

As he went by, everyone started to chase after him because they were sure there was no way he was going to make the turn.

Sure enough, he didn't make it. The car became airborne, flipped and barrel-rolled across the field.

By the time everyone got to the overturned car, the steam and smoke were pouring out of every opening.

Daddy thought the car was on fire and he was frantically trying to get out the window.

The only problem was that he had forgotten to unfasten his safety harness and he was about to pull himself in two.

He was not injured, but that was the end of Daddy's ever owning or driving a race car.

He said it was safer and cheaper to go to the races as a spectator.

THE GREEN FLAG
JUST MINUTES AWAY

My father, Wade Crider, was also a jokester, and he pulled a gag on me that nearly knocked me for a loop. He knew I could handle it, but he was prepared to step in if the gag got out of control.

After all, this was just minutes before the start of the Daytona 500, when I was paged on the public address system, "Curtis Crider, go to the telephone booth in the garage area."

When I picked up the telephone, my father said, "Son, your wife's in jail."

"Oh, my God." I was thinking the cars are lined up on pit road and the race will soon start. "Daddy, what's happening?"

"Well, she ran over a policeman."

"Oh, my goodness. Was he walking or in a car or what?"

"He was walking. He's not hurt bad, but they took your wife downtown to the jail."

I thought a minute, and I could hear the crowd cheering in the background. "I'll tell you what, Pop, she's just going to have to stay there until this race is over, because there's no way I can get a relief driver before the race starts, and there is no way I could get to town and back in time."

Like I said, my Dad knew I could handle it one way or the other. I went ahead and ran the Daytona 500 race.

After the race, my father and my wife were all there in the garage area and they let me in on the gag, which really had a basis in fact.

As my folks were coming into the Speedway grounds and the parking area, there was a tremendous traffic jam and much confusion.

Three or four policemen were trying to get the pedestrians off the road and into the infield area. One officer motioned to my wife to stop. Which she did. He stepped in front of her car.

Moments later, another officer, not seeing the policeman in front of the car in the excitement, stuck his head close to the window, blew his whistle and shouted to my wife to go ahead and make the turn.

Instinctively, Mary Frances obeyed the officer just inches away from her face, put the car in gear and bumped the policeman in front of her car.

She didn't knock him down, realizing quickly what was happening.

Of course, the officer was upset, but the two policemen talked a couple of minutes and agreed that it wasn't my wife's fault, so they let her continue into the infield.

After everyone recovered their composure, my father decided to rib me.

MY MOTHER, MUSIE CRIDER

Too little is said or written about a very important part of our sport, and our lives, the mothers of the racing people.

In our sport, most of the drivers start early in life, long before they are married with homes of their own, so they live at home.

There are hazards in every sport, hazards in auto racing, so it is the mother who stays up nights waiting for son to come back from a long night's racing trip far from home.

She worries when she is home waiting. When she is at the track watching, she has that feeling of impending danger, but she never shows it.

Although Mother may be concerned, she will never discourage her children from pursuing their chosen vocation.

In my case, Musie "Mama Boots" Crider was a great racing fan and she encouraged me. We had some great times together.

At Winston-Salem, N.C., Bowman Gray Stadium one night, I was roaring down the backstretch on the first lap and accidentally put my foot on the clutch pedal instead of the brake pedal.

As I went into the corner, I mashed what I thought was the brake and instead of slowing down, the car speeded up, free wheeling. Right through the little guard rail it went.

My mother had just told Dad about her concern and he said, "Oh, nothing's ever going to happen to him."

Mother told me later, no sooner than he had said that, than he saw my car go through the guard rail. "Down the grandstand he went, taking three or four steps at a time to get to you at the fence."

At another race in Danville, Va., my car rolled over and was lying on its side close to the fence that separated the race track from the grandstand area.

I unhooked the seat harness and climbed through the window above me. I was facing the crowd as I climbed out the window and there was Mother standing at the fence. I could almost shake hands with her. She had come out of the stand to the fence to be sure I was all right.

In later years, after the folks had moved to Richmond, she lived close to the Fairgrounds Speedway. She would always bring food to the track, chicken and sandwiches, and she would stand at the fence talking with me, my crew and the other racers there.

She thought they were the greatest people in the world and they thought much of her.

When Mother died in 1965, Cale Yarborough was a pallbearer. She would have liked that. Cale and his family sent flowers and he went to Greensboro where the funeral was held.

RACING FANS, BLESS THEM ALL

I'd like to talk to you about the racing fans. Each of you has your own stories about how you became racing fans.

There was one man, close to me, who resisted becoming a fan for a long time.

John Robert Wilson, Abbeville, S.C., was a mechanic and worked in automobile dealerships in his area. He was one of the best mechanics around.

Not all automobile mechanics are racing fans, not even this man, who had a racing driver as a son-in-law. Me.

I tried every way I could think of to get him to go to a race with Mary Frances and me, but he would always say things like, "Shucks, something's liable to fly off one of those race cars and come up in the grandstand or the pits and injure or kill somebody."

John Robert could not picture automobiles, which he figured were designed to carry family passengers, being used for a sport.

As we prepared for a race, all my men had gone on ahead to the track, and I was going to tow the race car and meet them there.

Mary Frances and I decided to pull a little trick on her father and I said, "John Robert, I don't know what I am going to do. I have to go to Aiken, S.C., to race this afternoon and I don't have any mechanic, nobody to go with me. I sure do wish you would go with me."

Always the gentleman willing to help a person in need, John Robert finally said, "Well, okay. Under those circumstances, I will go, but I don't want to see anyone get hurt."

We rode to Aiken together and he got so excited that he really didn't realize that my crew was already there. He probably thought they were some friends I had drafted on the spot.

Regardless, he was so thrilled and happy about auto racing when he saw it up close and personal that he became one of the most avid racing fans in that section of the country.

Every race, whether I was there or not, John Robert would be among the first at the pit gate, waiting for them to open up so he could see the race.

That is just one indication about the manner in which race fans become addicted to our sport.

Some, especially those who are mechanically inclined, become more involved, building race cars, such as Daddy did for a while.

Racing Action at Darlington, 1953. Junior Johnson, winner.

SHORT TRACK PROMOTERS
WITH THE P.T. BARNUM FLAIR

Around the Greenwood, S.C., area, two of the most active promoters were Lester Vanadore and Buddy Davenport. Working with them was Joe Hatchell, the flag man. Davenport did most of the public address announcing.

I can't say enough things about the short track promoters of those days because, regardless of the obstacles, they just kept going and kept the tracks running, kept auto racing available for the folks of the smaller cities and rural areas.

Some of the short track promoters of the '50s and '60s era are major operators today. Good examples of these would be Clay Earles at Martinsville, Va., Speedway and Paul Sawyer at the Richmond, Va., Fairgrounds Speedway.

The Martinsville Speedway is rated by news people and race fans far and wide as the most beautiful short track in the country, and Clay continues to improve it each year.

Paul Sawyer has been working hard for years to create a superspeedway in his Virginia area, but it hasn't been easy, with zoning and governmental requirements. Until then, Paul continues to operate the short track very successfully.

Lester Vanadore and Buddy Davenport were showmen of the "old school" style, carnies in a way, and just great. I know that many of the short track promoters had to take money out of their pockets to pay the purse on some rainy race days.

They were just great. They built racing, working with the drivers, car owners and pit crews. Yes, NASCAR officials, also.

Example, NASCAR's executive manager Pat Purcell was a

crusty veteran of sports and fair promotion from way back, in the '30s, a former newspaper sportswriter and manager of thrill shows and ice shows. There wasn't much that Purcell hadn't done before arriving at NASCAR.

He was a crafty fellow when dealing with cantankerous promoters.

In the NASCAR offices at 42 South Peninsula Drive, Daytona Beach, Vanadore would be debating the amount of a sanction fee.

Purcell would bring the discussion to an abrupt end. He wore a hearing aid which had, as normal in those days, the battery and controls in his shirt pocket.

Pat would deliberately reach over and turn off the hearing aid, then sit back and grin, "Go ahead, keep yelling. I can't hear a word."

Lester would sputter, then realize that he had been defeated, grin and reach for a pen to sign the sanction agreement.

Two master tacticians, each had something the other wanted. They only had to agree on terms. They wouldn't admit it, but both were satisfied with the ultimate deal.

Buddy Davenport was good as the track announcer, in his small track style.

He would dramatically instruct the flagman, Joe Hatchell, to "Hold them down 'til you see the whites of their eyes, then give them the green flag."

Can't you imagine Les Richter barking such an order before the Daytona 500? Yep, times have changed.

Buddy Davenport had a way of exciting the crowd even when there was no real action on the track, especially during that tour of England. His Southern grits style was completely new to those folks, who were a bit more on the conservative side.

Give Buddy two race cars practicing on the track, making some barking, crackling exhaust sounds and he could talk up a battle.

Those who were in line at the ticket window and listening to Davenport on the public address system were almost frantic in their desire to get into the stands and watch that action he was describing.

He would have the fans looking in both directions at once,

afraid they'd miss seeing something in the fourth turn or the first turn.

Buddy was a showman. Some critics said he was a ham, but he got the job done, excited the crowd and made them want to come back for the next race.

Davenport also proved himself to be an improviser at a NASCAR Modified and Sportsman cars mixed race in Columbia, S.C.

The drivers included such legends as Everett "Cotton" Owens, Alfred "Speedy" Thompson, his brother Jimmy Thompson, their father Bruce Thompson, and irrepressible Buddy Shuman.

The time trials session was a big thing with the fans. Very few of the crews had stop watches in those days, as compared to now when they all use sophisticated computers.

The mechanics would gear the cars based on their own experience, setting up for that particular track and that particular weather. Good educated guessing that more often worked fine.

Even without stop watches, the mechanics generally had a good built-in sense of timing and more than once they have disputed the calls by the stop watch-carrying timers.

Davenport discovered that he had forgotten to bring his own stop watches to the race track, so he improvised.

His style was always that he would poke his head and shoulders out the window of the timer's and announcer's stand and dramatically hold the watch in his hand and make the obvious motions of clicking the watch on and off, with over-emphasis.

This day, he palmed a silver dollar and went through the motions of pushing down the stem of the watch for every qualifying car.

He would flash the shining color of the coin so the competitors and the fans all thought it was a watch.

He had been carefully observing the cars in practice and he had time trialed so many in the past that he was accurate that night, so close to actual times that he didn't have a single dispute from a driver or mechanic.

A few shook their heads in disagreement with his calls, but no one demanded to see the watch as oft times would happen at other races.

It was a year later that Buddy finally told friends about that incident.

He explained that there was no time to send to his home for the watches, and to admit his error and have to draw numbers for starting positions, the fans would have been disappointed and some race teams would have been downright angry.

There are many times at races where it was necessary to draw numbers, such as because of a wet track or other condition, but forgetting to bring the watches from home would not constitute an emergency.

Davenport took a riverboat gamble and got away with it.

Curtis Turner in the '50s.

RUNAWAY RACE CAR
IN THE CORNFIELD

We were building a new race car in the shop in Charleston, S.C., so all but two of the guys stayed there while I went to Hillsboro, N.C., to race one Sunday.

The three of us took only what we absolutely needed for that race, and we even left the big truck back at the shop.

We were almost to Hillsboro, about 30 miles or so, just below Chapel Hill, when the tow bar broke loose from the pickup truck.

All racing fans know that a runaway race car, without a driver to control it, will turn left. Moments after I realized the tow bar had broken loose, I heard the safety chain snap. I could see in the rear view mirror that the race car was trying to run over the pickup truck, but was angling to the left side of that two lane road.

Coming toward us on that narrow road was a DeSoto and I could see the folks in that DeSoto, obviously a family enroute to church or a Sunday visit with family.

I held my breath as I waited for that race car to hit the DeSoto head-on, scared to death that someone would be hurt.

Fortunately, the runaway race car hit the DeSoto a glancing blow, mashing the fender against the front tire, crashing in the quarter panel and tearing off the door handles and the chrome strips along the side of the DeSoto.

The startled driver went down the road a bit, then parked. The race car made a left turn, knocked down a wire fence and stopped in the middle of a farmer's cornfield.

I stopped quickly and the three of us hurried back to the DeSoto to care for any injured there might be. Fortunately, no one was hurt, but they had been frightened half to death and they were all shook up about as bad as I was.

We pulled the fender away from the tire and talked with the man about the damage. He was a pretty good sport.

I asked, "How much damage do you think I did?"

"Well, I really don't know."

I added, "I sure don't either. I am a pretty fair mechanic, but I am not much on body work. How much was the car worth before I hit it?"

"Well, about $300, I reckon."

"I'll tell you what I will do. I'll just buy the car from you and you go ahead and drive it for a week or two until I get in touch with my Dad up in Greensboro," which was about 50 miles away.

"I'll get in touch with him, if he is not at the race track today, and get him to come over to your place and pick it up. You just go ahead and drive it."

The man said, "That's fine." I gave him the money and he gave me some papers sufficient to consummate the deal.

The farmer was standing outside his house. He had seen the whole commotion and he came over and said he would go get his tractor to pull the race car out of the cornfield.

Oh, boy, here comes the state policeman. "What's going on," he asked.

I told him, "Let me tell you something, this is the damnedest thing you have ever seen. My race car tore loose and hit my DeSoto."

The policeman turned to the DeSoto driver, "Is that right?"

"Yes sir, both of them is his. He owns both of them."

He couldn't figure out how a South Carolina race car could hit a North Carolina DeSoto, both headed in opposite directions. And me owning both of them. All this on a Sunday morning.

He shook his head, then said, "I'll tell you what, son. You keep that race car hooked up good from now on."

He drove away. No problem there.

After the farmer towed the race car out of the field, I asked, "How much do I owe you for the use of your tractor and for the damage to your cornfield?"

"Son, you don't owe me a thing. I haven't had as much fun and a good time on a Sunday morning in I don't know how long."

With everything hooked up again, we finally made it to the race track, but too late. The green flag for the race had already been waved and there was no way we could cross the track, unhook and join the race in progress.

We parked the pickup and the race car outside the track and walked down to the first turn to watch the race.

The folks at the gate, when they heard our tale, took pity and were kind enough to let us in free.

Curtis Turner won that race. I guess I was the big loser, but it could have been much worse if the DeSoto folks had been injured.

The thing that stands out in my memory of Curtis Turner is that every race he was in, or at least every race of his that I have seen, he was sure to go to the front of the field at some point.

If the equipment lasted or if he wasn't wrecked there was no other place for Turner but leading the race.

I'm sure I learned much about race driving just by watching Turner when I was on the sidelines. Sitting in a turn and just watching and remembering his techniques.

That Sunday in Hillsboro, I'm sure I gained knowledge just

watching Curtis drive, so the trip wasn't all wasted. Expensive, maybe, but not wasted.

After the race, we did not have to go through the work of loading up, because we had not unhooked the race car.

My sister Faye and brother-in-law Iva Perdue insisted that we go with them to their home in Greensboro, N.C. It wasn't that far out of the way, so we agreed to do that, then we would head back to Charleston.

Of course, because we were towing the race car, she beat us to the house. We arrived there about sundown.

Faye had already fixed up a big old supper of chicken, potatoes and biscuits and all that good stuff.

We showered and cleaned up and then had a great meal. We had been through a rough day and had not eaten at all.

Then Faye said to the three of us, "Okay, boys, you're all going to bed now."

I couldn't believe it. Going to bed that early in the evening. No way. We had to return to Charleston. There was work to be done on the new race car the next morning.

She insisted. Sis was the boss. There was no other way. We had to do what Faye said. The two guys with me said they would go along with whatever I decided.

Faye really knew what she was talking about because the three of us really slept, about 12 hours straight through. I didn't know a thing until about 8 or 9 o'clock Monday morning.

Really, I never felt so good in my life. We must have been exhausted and too dumb to know it. Faye could see the signs.

We had all been running a lot, getting three or four hours of sleep here, more work there and a few hours of sack time. This had been going on for weeks, and Faye accurately read the signs.

BUDDY BAKER, CURTIS CRIDER AND THE ENGINELESS RACE CAR

In the early '60s, it was time again for the NASCAR New England Tour, first stop Old Bridge, N.J. Buddy Baker was between rides for a short period, so he was to drive my second race car on the Northern Tour.

My crew had gone on to New Jersey with the equipment and the two race cars, and Buddy and I were driving up there in Buddy's passenger automobile.

While going through Virginia enroute, we decided to stop off in Washington, D.C., and look up Ratus Walters at his Cafe Burgundy.

Ratus owned the race car with which Larry Frank had won the 1962 Darlington Southern 500.

After visiting with us at his restaurant, Ratus invited us to go out in the country and see his place.

In the garage was his '62 Ford race car, sitting there without an engine. Everything else was intact, radiator and all.

Ratus said he was so busy that he didn't have time to race any more and he had sold off everything but the race car. We made a deal and bought the car from Ratus. Together we fashioned a tow bar in his well-equipped shop, and hooked it up behind Buddy's passenger car.

We figured we would tow the car to Old Bridge or until I could buy another car or truck to pull it. We would get an engine someplace.

At Old Bridge, Buddy and I qualified our race cars okay.

Ratus Walters' car was still hooked up to Baker's automobile.

As the cars were fueled and pushed to the straightaway, Baker and I noticed that all the cars were gone from the pits and there was still one place left vacant in the starting field.

The promoter had advertised a certain number of cars for that race and he was one short. The spectators notice things like that.

Buddy looked at me and smiled and I looked at him and grinned. We both had the same bright idea at the same time.

"Why not?" we asked.

One of our crew men got a spare helmet from the truck. Because we had lowered the front of the race car, to level it out for towing since there was no engine weight, with the radiator in place and the hood fastened, there was no indication to anyone that there was no engine in it.

We pushed the Walters car onto the track and lined up at the tail end of the field, seemingly ready to go.

I went back to the wrecker tow trucks and asked one of the drivers if he would mind pushing our car for a start as we were having a little trouble getting it fired. He said, "Not at all," that's what he was there for, to help teams with car trouble.

With one of our pit crew in the driver's seat, I told him, "When you go past the flagstand and the grandstand and the scoring stand as the wrecker truck is pushing you, just flip the switches and appear to do anything to start the engine.

"They won't start the race until that wrecker is off the track, so let him push you a full lap, then coast in behind the pit wall, throw your helmet down in disgust when you get out, get mad, maybe cry a little, kick the tires, whatever."

Sure enough, the wrecker driver pushed him a lap, my man dove behind the wall and went through all the motions of a disgusted driver.

We were paid for the last place finish with that car.

Buddy and I hadn't cheated anybody. The promoter had advertised a full field of cars and he got them. The money had already been set aside for that number of cars, so no other driver was shortchanged.

By the time we had arrived at the next race, Islip, Long Island, N.Y., the word had moved fast and we took a lot of kidding.

Another riverboat gamble, and it had worked.

Pat Purcell would probably have turned off his hearing aid if anybody had complained to him. He always liked a good joke, too.

The Winning Team of Cotton Owens and Buddy Baker.

Cotton Owens, Ralph Moody and Miss Pure Oil, 1954.

THE WORST WRECK EVER
IN THE ISLIP INFIELD

On arrival in Islip I went to the Mercury dealership where there was a wrecked station wagon, a new one that had been rear-ended, so I bought the engine from it and we installed that engine in Ratus Walters' '62 Ford.

Now, Buddy Baker and I had three cars for that Grand National tour.

During the race on that little quarter-mile asphalt track, a car in front of me lost the rear end cooler hose and it sprayed the track in front of me and covered my windshield with grease.

When the grease hit the windshield it literally "put out the lights." I couldn't see a thing.

A driver never wants to lock up the brakes when going through an oil slick, because the sliding tires will speed up the car and it will be out of control.

I couldn't see a thing and I knew that wall was out there. It seemed like I slid for 40 miles, but regardless I found the wall and it cleaned out the front end of the race car. I managed to let the car roll around into the infield.

When they restarted the race, the rear end was pointed toward the second turn. I was sitting on the hood with my back against the windshield. Lee Petty and some others were leaning against the front of the car, sort of watching the race.

A couple of cars got crossed up in that second turn area and one of the cars was spinning through the infield, headed right for my battered car.

As I had my back to that turn, I didn't see it coming, but when Petty and the others started running south, I knew something was coming from the north.

All I could do was flatten myself on the hood and hope for the best.

That car hit hard and it rolled the rear deck lid of my race car right up and over the top of my car. I never saw such a mess for a car parked quietly in the infield.

Fortunately, I escaped without any physical damage.

CURTIS CRIDER
AND MARVIN PANCH
GET TANGLED UP

It wasn't difficult to sign another driver for the third car, the '62 Ford Darlington winner with the new Mercury engine acquired from a dealer's junkyard.

All three of us had qualified for the Islip race and that Ford finished well enough to show me a profit and help us on the way to the next race, even though my own car was crunched. It really was a day-to-day existence, but we enjoyed it.

Those of us racing in that era worked long hours and we worked hard and dirty, but as we used to say, racing was better than working.

What we meant, of course, was that auto racing, with all its hard labor and long hours, was more interesting and challenging than an 8 a.m. to 5 p.m. job whether in an office, store or factory.

Also, we had independence. We made our own decisions, win or lose.

That engine I had purchased from the Mercury dealer in Islip was, most fortunately, one of the 352 cubic inch displacement engines with high performance headers on it, 360 horsepower.

I told the driver to stay out of trouble, put on a show and do the best he could, but don't crunch it!

Perhaps that was the hot tip, because he did okay.

Our schedule brought us up to Sag Harbor, away out east near the tip of Long Island, New York. We were to race on a road course.

The promoters had made arrangements for us to stay at a resort which had been converted from an old house which had been built by a whaling ship captain, and I do mean *old* house.

A beautiful place. Back in those days, accommodations for weekend visitors on Long Island were limited.

Buddy and I drove up in the front yard driveway and looked at this big, beautiful old place. Immediately, I saw a drawback and pointed out to Baker this was a big, three story house, built entirely of wood, surrounded by huge trees and overhanging branches.

"My God, Buddy. They put all of us in that place, what's going to happen if the place catches on fire during the night?"

The main hallway had been converted into a lobby. As we were among the early arrivals, I suggested that Buddy and I go upstairs quickly and pick out a room.

We opened many doors and looked over the rooms until we found the one that suited us, a big old tree right outside the window, with big strong limbs really close. If something did happen during the night, we could scramble out the window and down the tree to safety.

Our concerns were for nothing, because there was no fire, thank goodness, but years of travelling around had taught us to be cautious.

The place even had a nice recreation area downstairs with a ping pong table and a pool table, and the racers put them to good use the night before the race. There is not a lot of night life out there on Long Island, at least not the Southern style night life one found around Richmond and Darlington and Atlanta.

Because my regular race car was not yet repaired from the crash at Islip, I was driving the ex-Ratus Walters Ford at Sag Harbor.

During the race, Marvin Panch and I got our cars tangled up on one of the S curves of that road course backstretch and let me tell you we were doing figure eights side by side for about a mile and a half, and at high speed, down through an area of little scrub trees and shale dirt that covered the off-course infield.

We did not have windows in our race cars and the dust and stones and branches off the trees were flying into the cars. We were spinning in a complete cloud cover of dust, but every once in a while I would see Marvin face to face and the next moment I would be looking at the back end of his car.

We ended our wild rides side by side, close enough that I could have reached out and touched his car if I had been in a mood to do so. Believe me, we were both too busy for that.

My engine had choked down and I couldn't get it restarted.

I could look down and see that Marvin's car had its right front fender jammed in against the tire. His engine was still running, so I climbed out, pulled the fender off his tire and checked the other three wheels.

Everything looked okay, so I signaled to Marvin to get going, and he was off and running, back into the fray.

There my car sat with a stalled engine, well off the track backstretch, so they were not stopping the race. In fact, I don't think they had even missed me yet.

There were two security guards at a gate nearby so I called to them, "Hey, how about letting some of the spectators out here and giving me a push to start the car?"

"No, we can't do that, but if we can get you down there and inside the gate, then they can push you all they want to."

"Okay, let's us three try it."

The two men really pitched in. We pushed the car back and, fortunately, it was on a downhill grade and we were close to the gate.

The car was rolling, they opened the gate, and in the car went.

I climbed in, buckled up and I'll bet there were 300 spectators wanting to get their hands on that race car and push.

Of course, there wasn't room for 300, but enough of them pushed and the engine fired. I turned the car around and back out the gate I went, onto the race course.

Every time I drove down that backstretch there was a mob of people cheering and clapping and waving. They now had a piece of that race car and I had my own cheering section right there.

Marvin Panch and I both finished the race in the top ten positions, even after all that mess.

Before I leave the saga of the '62 Ford, I want to point out that whenever a car owner or a builder such as Ratus Walters drops our of racing, because of the press of business or whatever reason, it is a great loss to racing as a whole. They are such great people, we are all family, especially in stock car racing.

TINY LUND GAVE GOOD ADVICE

One of the advantages to being a touring professional racing driver in the good ole days was meeting so many nice people and forming long-standing friendships, not just man to man, but families also.

Trips to Heidelberg, Pa., Speedway included visits with Nick Garin and his wonderful family and friends who lived at nearby McDonald, Pa. The friendship was nurtured during a race at Heidelberg and lasted throughout the years. Whenever Nick and his family would come to Daytona Beach, they would visit with us.

There was a time a couple decades ago when Nick telephoned to say he wanted to buy a race car, so I sold him one of my Grand National cars.

The deal was that I would bring it to Heidelberg and drive it in a race. He owned the car, win, lose or whatever, but naturally I wanted to win the first race for him.

Because this would be a quick trip back home since I had to get another car ready for my next race, my wife and two children and I towed the race car with our family passenger car, leaving the truck at home.

Everything was going great during the race, and I was feeling proud and happy for what I was showing Garin. We had a good shot at winning. That is, until the final pit stop, which was a quick one, everything great.

Anxious as I left the pit, I over-revved the engine and by the time I reached the number one turn, the engine had dropped a valve. We were out of the race.

Tiny Lund at Daytona, 1967.

Of course, I was not the first driver, nor will I be the last, to make that mistake, but that fact is little consolation.

Nick had been around racing a long time and he was a good sport, accepting that as what we call "that's racing."

Before he had bought my race car, Nick and his family would take us over to his house and feed us and give us a place to stay. He couldn't do enough for us and we enjoyed being with the Garins.

That race day, of course, we had to hurry back home, but Nick has continued to play host to us through the years.

Later, after the Heidelberg race, Nick telephoned me in Charleston to say that he had a new car built and he wanted to run it at Lancaster Speedway, a dirt track which had recently been paved. He wanted me to drive the car.

At Lancaster, we could not get that car to run properly, no matter what we did. We would practice during the day, then at night, cold as it was, we would take the car to a local garage and dismantle the whole front end, the A frames, everything.

The next day it was just like driving a 16-foot long two by four piece of wood.

I would get it in a corner and it just would not turn left. The car wanted to go straight ahead. We couldn't stop it from pushing no matter what changes we made.

Tiny Lund had been watching me those days and he walked over to where Nick and I were scratching our heads and he quietly said, "Curtis, if that car isn't handling right, just don't drive it." He didn't have to tell us that the Lancaster track had a reputation for being a tough track, hard on cars and drivers.

Nick and I talked it over. We worked on the car right up to the last minute. It wouldn't handle. It wouldn't run fast enough. We both agreed it was not safe to race, so Nick loaded it back up and we watched the race, a couple of unhappy spectators.

But, as goes the cliche, "That's racing!"

North Wilkesboro, 1953

Jimmy Thompson in a 1955 Pontiac.

CURTIS GOT A CHARGE
FROM DICK HUTCHERSON

T he Darlington, S.C., Southern 500, 1957, came up on the schedule and even though I didn't have a Grand National car, I wasn't going to miss that grand-daddy of a race.

There was a major traffic jam of fans and competitors trying to go into the tunnel to the infield.

Bobby Myers and his crew were in line up front, so I walked up to them and rode in with them.

Myers was pitting on the backstretch, just before the third turn.

As I roamed around the pit area, just a few pits from Bobby Myers was a newcomer to Grand National, Dick Hutcherson, from the tall corn Iowa country.

Hutcherson had been a star on the IMCA (International Motor Contest Association) on the central states' fairgrounds circuit, and a great person. He is still active in NASCAR today, building Grand National (Winston Cup) race cars in Charlotte, N.C.

I talked with Dick and his crew and sort of hung around his pit.

Also, sadly, that was the last time I talked with Bobby Myers. During that race, Myers' and Fonty Flock's cars crashed and Bobby was fatally injured.

As mentioned, I stayed around the Hutcherson crew. Dick had a '57 Ford.

As Hutcherson and the field came down the front stretch and the starter waved the green flag, Dick's car engine shut off completely. He coasted around to his pit. The crew had the hood up and I pitched in to help. In no time, I felt like I was part of the crew.

Dick had no idea what had caused the engine to quit. We had no diagnostic equipment and we wouldn't have had room to use it if we had it.

I pulled the coil wire out and stuck my finger up in the opening and motioned for Dick to turn over the engine. I was sure I would get a good jolt of electricity, but nothing happened. There was no spark at all.

So I told the crew members to get me a set of points, a condenser and a coil in a hurry. I had the cap off and looked in there, but could see nothing wrong.

As the crew members brought tools, I took charge, put in the new points and the condenser, then stuck my finger in the coil and told Dick to try the starter again.

I got a jolt that time, a good one, that almost knocked off my socks.

I put the distributor cap back on, buttoned up the hood and Dick fired it up.

With all that work, Hutcherson had lost only twelve laps. He finished that race and continued to have some good seasons of Grand National racing. A popular man, whose skill and charisma have paid off with his race car building for some of the best teams in NASCAR today, other circuits as well.

CURTIS TURNER, LITTLE JOE WEATHERLY AND THE MONGOOSE

We were not always serious around the race tracks. As we used to say, "We don't make much money, but we have a lot of fun."

I had a pet mongoose which I carried around to some of the tracks in a wooden box with a wire covering and a door in one end, a pretty good cage.

The box was lettered with warnings such as, "Beware! Stay Back!" and "Poisonous Animal."

First, a mongoose is not a poisonous animal, and second, there was no mongoose, just an illusion.

Fastened on the inside to the spring-loaded trap door on the end of the cage was a fox tail, the novelty store variety which folks used to hang on their auto antennas. I had a string fastened to a trigger to release the trap door lock.

A few curious people would gather around, peek into the cage and see a bit of fur and let their imaginations run wild. I would tell them to crouch down, scratch on the top of the box and the mongoose would think he was going to be fed and would be ready to come out.

At the appropriate moment I would tug on the string, the trap door would fly open and the fox tail would whip up and out, almost brushing the victim's face.

It was a dirty trick in a way, but after folks got over the momentary start, they laughed and went looking for some other friends to induct into the gag.

I had a crowd around the cage at Darlington one day,

almost ready to spring the trap, when Curtis Turner and some friends walked by.

Curtis did not know about the gag, but he could see the bushy tail inside and he said, "Wait a minute. That's no mongoose. A mongoose has a slick tail. They don't have fur on them like that."

I wasn't about to let Curtis mess up my trick. In fact, I wanted to catch him, also.

I said to Turner, "Well, to tell you the truth, Curtis, I don't really know what kind of an animal that is. Do you want to get him out of there and we'll find out?"

Turner said, "Well, you just get him out of there and I'll tell you what it is. I know it ain't no mongoose."

I said, "Scratch on that end of the box and we'll get him to come out."

Turner was bending down and sort of squatting, and he got really interested, waiting for the animal to come out.

I pulled the string, the trap door flew open and the fox tail flailed the air. I jumped and yelled, "Look out! He's loose!"

Everyone started running. Turner jumped up, turned and started to run from the box.

A lady who had bent over his shoulder tried to back away and she and Turner were moving away face to face.

In a few moments, folks caught on and started coming back, howling with laughter, some with embarrassed laughter at being so gullible.

Curtis Turner told me it about scared him half to death, this one of the most daring men to ever drive a race car.

Little Joe Weatherly had come along just about at the punch line and after he saw what the gag had done to Turner, he took great delight in hunting up unsuspecting newspaper reporters, broadcasters and sponsors and bringing them to me one or two at a time for me to "show them the mongoose."

Weatherly was quite a jokester himself, and it tickled him to be a contributing participant.

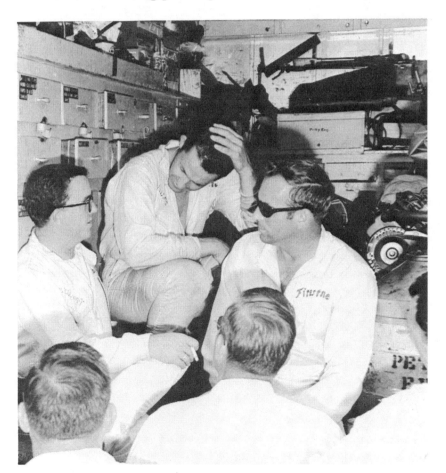

Sam McQuagg, Richard Petty and Friends.

CURTIS CRIDER
CONVINCES THE BANKERS

In 1962, some of the superspeedway promoters worked on a plan to attract a variety of automobiles competing in their races by offering bonuses of $1,000 each for the best finish by any make of car.

Example, if Fords finished one-two, a couple of Pontiacs next and a Plymouth fifth, the $1,000 each would go to the winning Ford, the third place Pontiac and the fifth place Plymouth, and on down the line to the best finishing Mercury, Chevrolet, Chrysler and Dodge. Those were the prominent brands of automobiles racing NASCAR Grand National that year.

There was one stipulation, to win the award the car must have gone at least half the race distance.

I had an older car and felt that I could do better if I updated my equipment. I wanted to buy a '62 Mercury.

As I was living in Charleston, S.C., I went to what I considered to be my bank and explained my need for a loan.

The bankers listened, took it under consideration, and a short time later told me that being a race driver, they did not think I was gainfully employed sufficiently to borrow that kind of money to buy an automobile.

I telephoned Bob Calvin, the president of the Darlington Raceway, and outlined my problem. He said, "Curtis, why don't you come up here and we'll talk about it."

Calvin never told me whether he had talked to his bankers,

but it is quite obvious that he had done so. I went to his bank as he suggested, laid the plan on the table for the people, what I planned to do with the money, and the potential for the bonus money.

The Darlington bank lent me a third of the money I needed. Next I went to banks in Abbeville and Savannah, Ga., getting a third from each. They were each aware of what the other banks were doing, all on signature loans.

It was also obvious that the men in those three banks were racing fans. In fact, in each bank, we talked more about racing than we did about my financial statement.

I went to the Mercury dealer in Charleston and paid cash for a '62 Mercury. It had 13 miles on it when I drove it to the shop.

Boy, did we hustle to get that car ready for the Charlotte race.

We qualified well. There were three Mercurys which had factory support, so they were my biggest threat. I had to get ahead of those three, finish ahead of those three, and of course, go more than halfway to earn the $1,000 bonus, plus whatever purse I could earn normally.

My luck was running good that day, because each of those three factory supported Mercurys went out with various ailments. I felt sure that the other Mercury entries had also failed, or were about to do so.

Then, approaching the halfway mark, my troubles began, rear axle trouble, that is, and it began to smoke.

I stayed on the track as long as I could, staying out of the way of other cars, just adding laps, because I had to reach halfway.

Eventually the condition worsened and I had to park the race car behind the pit wall, then push to the garage area.

I was afraid that I had not reached halfway, although I knew the race leaders had done so.

I literally ran to the scoring stand and after checking, sure enough, I had passed halfway and was the last Mercury running, so I had won the $1,000 bonus.

So, along with the prize money I won for qualifying and finishing position in that and the remaining races, I had enough to repay the three banks. I had good equipment ready for the rest of the season, too.

The 1962 season was quite good for me. I finished 12th in the Grand National point standings ahead of such stalwarts as Buck Baker, Bob Welborn and Junior Johnson. I was in 52 races, had three top five place finishes and was in the top ten 18 times, earning $9,540 in race day purses, plus seasonal point money and other payments.

One item of note, especially this year when Dale Earnhardt is the reigning Winston Cup National Champion, well earned. In 1962, his father, the late Ralph Earnhardt was 29th in the point standings, one spot ahead of Cotton Owens. I was in elite company that year.

Sportsman-Modifieds, mid 1950s.

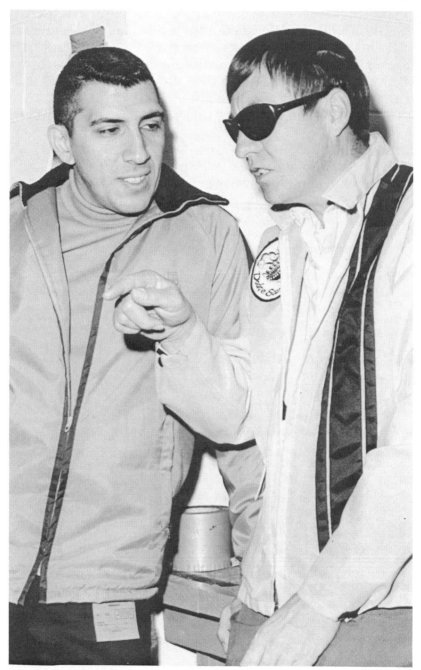

Don Naman and Bobby Isaac.

RACERS DO HAVE TIME FOR RECREATION

There is an inherent danger about auto racing. The drivers know it. The mechanics know it and the officials know it. The families of the drivers know it, but they don't talk about it, don't even admit it to themselves.

If a driver was afraid, he would never accomplish anything on the race track. The knowledge is there, however, and perhaps that stops him from doing something stupid on the track.

NASCAR officials have always been concerned about maintaining safety. The cars are safe. The tracks are much safer today than they were in my days, because we all learn and profit from experience.

Indy 500 driver Ray Haroun invented the rear view mirror and Goodyear invented the safety inner cell for gasoline tanks, greatly reducing the danger of fire, and NASCAR introduced the netting at the driver's side window.

Yes, stock car racing is safer than ever.

Drivers will tell you that they feel safer on the speedway than they do driving from the hotel to the track.

Then there are the hazards while engaged in recreation.

Let me tell you about my daughter Jan and the golf cart. She was a living doll from the day she was born.

One day when I was practicing my golf game at the Berkeley Country Club in Monks Corner, S.C., Jan went along to ride in the golf cart.

She watched me drive it and work the controls, then she started to drive to where the ball had fallen. I would get out, hit the ball and get back in and we would go to the next spot on the course. Nothing unusual about that.

At one point we were on a hillside, with a ditch at the bottom. I didn't want to hit the ball into that ditch, so I stroked it easily. The ball rolled only a short distance, so I walked down the hill to it for the next stroke.

Jan was sitting in the cart at the top of the hill, so I motioned for her to come on down.

My back was to her and the cart as I lined up the ball for the next stroke to the green. I heard a noise. I guess she screamed. The cart was careening down the hill right toward me, with the ditch in front of me and almost no place to hide.

One way or another, Jan got the cart stopped and under control, and I was able to jump to one side, so no damage was done except to frighten both of us.

We were kidding about it later, wouldn't it have been ironic that I would race on some of the toughest dirt tracks in the country and tour England with a race car, then get run over by a golf cart on my own home golf course?

Curtis in 1972. Daughter Jan at right rear of car.

You are probably wondering, if you have followed some of this narration, how we happened to be playing golf in Monks Corner when we lived in Charleston and I had my racing garage there, too.

One Sunday morning at the breakfast table my wife read a newspaper advertisement. "Lookit here, they are having some kind of a deal going on up at that Berkeley Country Club in Monks Corner. Let's ride up there. They're having a big deal and a free barbecue."

As it was only about 18 miles away, and I wasn't racing that Sunday, why not? Free barbecue sounded okay.

On arrival we learned that the event was a promotion for selling houses at that country club, and, would you believe, we ended up buying a three bedroom brick house.

So, you see, advertising and promotion does pay, and we were never sorry we did it.

My auto racing experience included more than building race cars and driving them. I also have done some auto racing promoting, for a while at the Cooper River Speedway, just north of Charleston and south of Monks Corner, associated with a good friend, Mr. Powers.

My son Chip was 10 or 11 years old during that period and even at that tender age he had more laps around that race track than most of the drivers.

Why? Because he drove the water truck, filling the truck tank with water, then riding lap after lap wetting down the dirt surface to eliminate a dust problem during the races.

One time in the mid-1960s, we decided to hold a bicycle race at the speedway for the children between eight and 15 years of age, a community service thing which is good for all business ventures.

It went over great, the parents were delighted and there were many more entries than we had anticipated. We were enthusiastic.

It was agreed the race would be for ten laps around the track, about 2 1/2 miles.

I was flagging the race and after three laps, some of the younger kids began to drop out. It was apparent that ten laps would be too long a distance, so I made a quick decision to cut the race to little more than half.

I held up two fingers as the boys and girls came around on

the fourth lap and as most were racing fans, they knew that the flagman signaled that way to drivers near the end of the race.

They accepted the two-lap signal, then got the white flag the next time around and finally the checkered flag.

I was quite pleased with myself. Everything had worked out great, until Chip stopped his bike at the flagman's stand and looked up at me.

I have never seen a young man as angry as Chip was.

"Daddy, why did you do that?!?"

"Well, Chip, we had to cut it short because some of the younger kids were getting tired and we realized they could not go the distance."

"I know! That's why I was running in 12th place, just cooling it so I would be strong the last five laps, and you called it off at the halfway point. I don't like that!"

I realized immediately that Chip had made a good point, and I have recalled that incident many times at auto races.

Officials have to make snap decisions because of track conditions or weather or whatever, and more than a few times, those changes in plans have been costly to the planning on one team or another.

Drivers and crews plan their race strategy in advance and when the signals are changed by officials, even when it is unavoidable, the best laid plans are trashed and races are won or lost.

"It isn't fair," the handicapped race crews complain, but then, who ever said life was fair? A fella just has to roll with the punches, as Chip learned that day.

His feelings were damaged, but he did not bear any psychological scars. Boys do have a way of bouncing back.

MOONSHINING
AND STOCK CAR RACING

In today's high tech world and with the Madison Avenue influence, some folks want to put behind them the memory of earlier days when moonshining and stock car racing were intertwined.

Regardless, no story about stock car racing is complete without some honest reflection.

In the '40s, '50s and '60s (and of course long before that), moonshining was a way of life. The guys who were doing it did not want to hurt anyone, and neither did the "revenooers" of the day.

Louis Jerome "Red" Vogt, the ace of auto racing engine builders and the man who gave NASCAR its name, a member of the Stock Car Auto Racing Hall of Fame, owned a garage in Atlanta. He built the moonshine runners' cars in one section of the garage and the revenuers' cars in another area. Never the twain should meet.

Vogt smilingly refuses, even today, to answer the question whether he did anything different with one set of engines than the other.

Regardless, the moonshine runners and the revenue officers worked together in competition, but without personal rancor. It was a way of life for all of them.

My good friend Junior Johnson, the man they once dubbed The Last American Hero and also a Hall of Famer, once was caught tending his father's still, and just a few years ago, President Ronald Reagan issued him an official pardon.

My brother Ike and I did our share of moonshine running, the words they have used to describe hauling the liquor from the still to market.

One of my most harrowing experiences came after I had picked up nine or ten cases of liquor in Greenwood, S.C., scheduled for Abbeville delivery. After that, we were going to race in Aiken, S.C. The liquor was stored up front in the truck with which we would pull the race car.

We piled some cases of oil, the gas cans and some tires and tools on top of the liquor cases.

We looked all over Abbeville that Saturday night, but couldn't locate the customer, and thus could not unload the liquor.

Oh, well, we just had to roll on to Aiken for the race the next day, a Sunday.

At that time, I was driving a race car for Cecil and Athel Yon of Charleston. I would keep the race car with me from track to track until it needed repairs, then go back to Charleston for the work.

At Aiken everything worked okay until late in the race when the race car developed engine problems.

Charleston was closer than Abbeville, so first things must come first, get the race car repaired. Take care of the whiskey delivery later.

We checked in at the Yon Brothers Garage and I told Cecil, "I have some whiskey on that truck and I've got to get rid of it."

Cecil said he would make a phone call or two, and he did. I talked to the people, told them how much we had and it all sounded pretty good.

The buyers would come to the garage, taste the whiskey to be sure it was okay and then take it off my hands, at least out of my truck. But they didn't show.

It was getting late and we decided to give up on it that day and go to the motel. We had unhooked the race car and we had the liquor in the truck, covered with the boxes of oil, tools and the tires.

On the way to the motel, the police stopped us. At first, I thought someone had tipped the police because we were cutting in on another distributor's territory, which was generally a no-no.

It was after sundown. We got out of the truck and walked back to the police car and the officers got out with their flashlights.

They were nice enough, but they were flashing the lights around at the stuff in the truck. I showed them my driver's license and tried to stay cool.

"Where did you get all those tires and wheels?"

Then I got the picture. They were not looking for whiskey. They thought we had ripped off a tire store or were stripping cars or something.

I explained quickly, "We're racing people. We race for the Yon Brothers Garage here in Charleston and we have been working on the race car there. We are just headed for the motel for the night."

The policeman threw the beam up toward the back of the truck and I could see one corner of a case of whiskey under the pile of tires and all.

Every time the light would aim towards the whiskey, I'd take his hand and move the light to another area. "Those are the kinds of tires we run on asphalt." I'd pull it to another side and say, "Those are the tires we run on dirt."

I gave him a lesson in auto racing there on the side of the road, whether he wanted it or not. They did seem to be interested.

Soon they were satisfied that we hadn't ripped off any cars, and then they received another call, so they told us to take it easy and wished us good luck.

I do want to interject here that there was a whole wide world of difference between whiskey running as it was many decades ago, and the narcotics trade which is so damaging today. The whiskey was being consumed by adults. It wasn't penetrating to the children and into the schools.

Eventually, as history tells us, Congress decided that the prohibition laws were a mistake and repealed them.

Moonshining was considered a harmless way of life back then. No right thinking person would say the same today about narcotics. Please don't ever confuse the two. President Reagan put the difference on the line when he pardoned a moonshiner, but works to strengthen the laws against illegal narcotics.

End of sermon.

I hauled a lot of whiskey even with the trunk of my '49 Ford coupe partially open.

The busiest months were November, December and January, holiday times, people stocking up for parties. You know what they used to say about the public in those days, "They vote dry, but they drink wet." It was true, many of the best of citizens, the civic leaders, enjoyed drinking whiskey at home or at private parties.

We got most of our stuff in Swansea and would haul it to the Greenwood area. Sometimes we would go to Columbia and pick up a load. There was no shortage of suppliers, no shortage of customers.

In December, we would throw the cases in the trunk, break off a cedar branch and stuff it on top of the whiskey, pull down the trunk lid and tie it tight with a rope.

We were hoping the police would figure we had been out gathering Christmas trees as we drove through those small towns, the cedar branches flapping in the wind.

There were Navy bases and Air Force bases around Charleston and Fort Jackson in Columbia, with G.I.s hitchhiking.

We'd pick up a couple to make it look like we were a bunch of soldiers travelling.

Once, just outside a small town, Ike was driving and we had

a sailor on the seat between us, talking and having a great time.

Suddenly, there was a police car across the road.

My brother looked at me as if to ask, "What do we do now?" I pointed to the police car and said, "Keep going and stop." I figured if we turned to run, they would know something was wrong and the police did have radios about that time.

As we eased up to the policeman, he said to Ike, "Y'all take it easy. There's a wreck up there around the curve."

Ike tried to hide his relief as he said, "Yes, sir. Thank you."

As we drove on, Ike and I both said, "Whew!" and the sailor gave us a funny look.

Guess he figured out what we were really doing. In fact, some of the sailors and soldiers were good customers for whiskey dealers.

Cotton Owens wins Daytona in 1953.

From Left: Jim Wilson, Harry Hill, Ray Fox, Junior Johnson. 1960.

"DON'T LET MY HUSBAND RACE!"

We were running a demolition derby type race at the Cooper River Speedway and I was flagging, wearing a set of headphones connected to the announcer in the tower. The announcer was Clarence Jackson.

About halfway into the race, Jackson received a telephone call from a lady in that area and she was excited, "Please don't let my husband get in that race. He left here with my brand new car and he swears that he's going to get in the race and win it."

They told me through the intercom about the phone call and just then I saw this new car coming out of the pit gate onto the race track.

No one was supposed to come through that gate during the race. We had people who were supposed to be tending the gate, but someone slipped up.

Here he came, up pit road and right onto the race track. Cars were going every which way, banging each other, but most of them missed the newcomer.

Jackson, still on the telephone with the distraught wife, said, "Lady, if it's a new Ford, I'm sorry but it's too late."

The intruder had let the car get out of control, one wheel up on the guard rail, wiping out the suspension, the radiator, everything up front. That new Ford was a mess.

I waved the red flag and the crews rushed out and got the cars stopped.

Because the man might have been injured, the ambulance was there quickly and so were the deputy sheriffs. When the

driver came out of the car, he was huge, probably the biggest man in the county, and had he ever been drinking!

The deputies finally got him under control, then he demanded to be paid for winning the race. He insisted he had won.

We got him to our little office and someone telephoned his wife, who got a neighbor to drive her to the race track.

We really could not have handled him, he was so huge, but his wife could and did. She picked him up and took him off and we could only guess about his later discomfort. She was one angry wife. We had our wrecker pick her once-new Ford off the guard rail and tow it to the infield where the man or the woman could have it hauled away Monday.

Clarence Jackson was a disc jockey at a Monks Corner radio station and a certified character. He had a running gag about his professed liking for buttermilk and green onions.

At the time for one of his normal promos on behalf of the track, he would urge the spectators to "go down to the concession stand and get you some hamburgers and hot dogs, something cold to drink. Be sure to try the buttermilk and green onions."

While the regulars were used to this line of patter, some people would actually try to order some buttermilk and green onions.

The concession sales people had to politely explain that there were none, it was just Clarence Jackson's little gag.

REMEMBERING BUDDY SHUMAN

Buddy Shuman and I raced as a team one day at the Greenwood, S.C., race track, about which you've heard earlier in this book.

It was a quarter-mile dirt oval, banked up around a football field, with grandstands on both sides, reminding one of Bowman Gray Stadium in Winston-Salem, N.C.

It was an ideal place to race, good clay surface, and the tires would really get a good bite. It was easy to maintain and Lester Vanadore and Buddy Davenport kept it in good shape.

Their opening race each season was a 500-lap team race. A Modified car and a Sportsman car would be a team, but only one of them on the track at a time. When one team member would pit for fuel or other needs, the other car would immediately go out into the race.

The driver waiting in the pit area had to keep his attention up in case of unscheduled pit stops. The moment one team car entered the pit area, the other fellow would have to charge out.

The year Shuman and I were a team, we were the race winners.

Another year, both Speedy Thompson and I elected to run without partners, the only two drivers to run the entire 500 laps single handed.

In that way, a fellow would not have to split the prize money. Running 500 laps on a quarter-mile track was a tiring chore, but if a fellow was money hungry enough, he could attempt it. Neither Speedy or I won that day, but we probably each made more money than if we had teamed up with others.

There was a day when I dropped by the Shuman and Thompson racing shop. Buddy was going to race a Modified car in Richmond, but Willie Thompson couldn't get away so he asked me to take his place as the one-man pit crew/crew chief or whatever.

The Shuman-Thompson cars were always strong. Cotton Owens and Fireball Roberts were among the competitors.

During the final practice session, Shuman said he was having right front brake problems. Every time he would go into a turn, the car would head straight toward the outside wall.

There was not sufficient time to pull off the big old safety hub.

I worked on the anchors on the bottom, backed off the adjustments and tried to relocate the anchors. With the type of brakes we were running, there was no way to determine the problem when the car was just sitting in the pit.

Soon it was time for the feature race so there was nothing Shuman could do but go out and hang on the best he could.

He would get into the lead, the brake would lock up if he had to stand on the binders in a turn and he would slide toward the wall and would be passed by two or three cars. Then he would have to fight to get back the lead.

Shuman finished fourth or fifth that day, and I felt bad because I was the only mechanic he had. I wondered if I had missed something.

A couple of days later, Willie Thompson told me what was the problem. A spring inside had broken. When Shuman applied the brakes, the shoe would go out against the drum, but with no spring, it wouldn't come back when he released the brake pedal until the pressure in the wheel cylinder was reduced gradually.

Later, I wished I had pulled a trick that racers did sometimes, put the race car out on the track, then pull the safety hub. They wouldn't have been able to start the race until I finished the repairs.

Just another case of a 15 cent item costing a team a race victory. How many times has it happened? Too many for those losers.

There are times when a break will occur at a fortunate moment. This was at a half-mile track in South Carolina and I had won the race.

As usual, we were gathered at the start/finish line for the trophy presentation and the photos.

I asked my son Chip, "Will you take the race car over to the infield now and put it on the trailer?"

Chip fired up the engine, pulled away, made a left turn into the pits and just about 12 feet later, the right rear hub and axle ran out about a foot or two from the side of the car.

The housing on the floater rear end had snapped, probably on the final turn of the final lap.

After slowing down, the car had made it around one more lap to the trophy presentation. I could only imagine the disaster if the break had occurred earlier, during the race, even the last couple of laps.

In the 1954 era, Ford Motor Company became more involved in stock car racing and Buddy Shuman was selected to head up their preparation of the cars for the NASCAR Grand National Series.

Previously he had been one of the top NASCAR technical inspectors, after retiring as a race driver.

In both positions, Shuman acquitted himself well, a truly memorable character whose name and exploits will live in the stock car racing history annals.

Tragically, one Saturday night before a race, Shuman died of smoke inhalation in a motel room fire, presumably started by a burning cigarette when he fell asleep.

Shuman must have smiled when he looked down on that funeral, with friends and associates gathered from Detroit to Miami, fans, pit crews, car owners, officials and competitor race drivers.

Dick McGeorge of Champion Spark Plug Co. created the Buddy Shuman Memorial Trophy to be presented annually to the person who made important contributions to stock car racing.

Even after McGeorge's passing, Champion has continued to honor the Shuman memory with the prestigious annual award.

Cotton Owens, 1958.

Bob Welborn, 1958, on the beach.

A LITTLE NITRO
GOES A LONG WAY

The word nitro sounds explosive, but nitromethane mixed with an engine fuel is not hazardous to anybody or anything but the engine itself, as far as I know.

Nitromethane or "pop" has been used for years, most extensively with the Indianapolis race cars. It is not allowed on today's Winston Cup circuit, where Unocal 76 racing gasoline is mandatory.

Bobby Myers was one of the best drivers in any class of racing and he was best known in the NASCAR Modified and Sportsman short track arenas.

In a slightly humorous situation one day, he had won the race and was receiving his honors in victory lane when a tire on his race car suddenly went flat, startling everyone around and providing a good laugh with the "what if?" comments.

There was a race at Savannah, Ga., when Bobby not only did not win but the result was downright embarrassing.

The fact that Bobby Myers and I had been partying quite a bit Saturday night before the race didn't have any bearing on his problems. We had gone uptown that evening and relaxed around with friends.

In those days it was permissible to use nitromethane additive with the gasoline in the Modified Sportsman race cars. Of course, it was necessary to have your engine set up precisely to burn nitro in small quantity. His car owner, Calvin Wooten, was a good builder and always had good equipment.

As they prepared for the race, Myers put a little nitro into the gasoline tank, the prescribed amount, as normal.

Without realizing that Bobby had already taken care of that little chore, Wooten commented, "I guess I'd better put in the nitro," and he did just that.

A short time later, along came the crew chief and, sure enough, he put in the volatile fuel additive.

When the green flag was waved, that race car took off like a jet.

It was unbelievably fast for a couple of laps and officials and crews in the pit area were astounded. You can imagine the feeling of fellow drivers as Myers opened a whopping lead on the field.

It all ended just as quickly when all the pistons in that engine melted.

As the crew members scratched their heads in bewilderment, they began to compare notes and only then did they discover the triple dosing of nitromethane.

CALE YARBOROUGH'S
SENSE OF HUMOR

Racing drivers and their pit crews are very serious people when they are preparing for a race, but you race fans have learned many times, when talking with your favorites after a race or on their personal appearance occasions, that they are witty, intelligent and regular folks, fun to listen to.

You have heard many times, and probably have seen the photograph, of the time Cale Yarborough's race car was airborne and went completely over the wall and outside the Darlington Raceway oval.

Fortunately Cale escaped serious injury and he was back inside the track after a while.

Naturally, Cale was the center of attention from the sportswriters and broadcasters, who wanted all the details.

"Well, it tore up the car pretty bad, but I'm all right. But the biggest thing about the whole incident," he continued, without a smile, "Bob Calvin (promoter and head of the raceway) wanted me to buy another ticket to get back in."

With all the Winston Cup races being broadcast by the Motor Racing Radio Network, and so many on television, drivers such as Dick Brooks, Benny Parsons, Phil Parsons and David Pearson are being used as color commentators on days when they are not competing on the asphalt.

It pays you to listen to them, because they provide a special kind of insight, and not always serious. They put a light touch on their commentaries, analyzing what is going on in the minds of the drivers and the crew chiefs at any given moment in the races.

I have reported to you about our trip to England. Bobby Myers almost got in a bit of trouble with a quip as we went through customs in New York City, enroute to England.

The customs inspector routinely asked Bobby how many pieces of luggage he had to declare.

"Fifty-four pieces, sir."

The customs man looked at him, "Fifty-four pieces? What are they?"

"A deck of cards and a pair of socks," replied Bobby with a grin.

The customs man showed his irritation, "Young man, this is serious business."

"Okay, sir. Two suitcases."

MORE LIGHTHEARTED CHATTER

At Boyd speedway in Chattanooga, Tenn., David Ethridge wandered into my pit area and we began chatting. He had just closed a gasoline station in Marysville, Tenn., and he was footloose and fancy free.

He appeared to be a good person so I suggested, "Why don't you just come on and join our pit crew and ride around the country a bit?"

We were running Grand National races once a week and we did need an extra person at the time.

The races in Nashville, Tenn., were a lot of fun because the Music City is a great town for visitors, plenty of good things to do with the various country music clubs and other fun spots.

Traditionally, the country singing stars have been auto racing fans and the racers have been country music fans. Remember the record albums the NASCAR drivers put out a couple of times? Marty Robbins was a good race driver and Kyle Petty had already started a career as a country singer. Bobby Allison and Darrell Waltrip and Kyle Petty have been guests on the Nashville Now television program several times in 1986.

The night before the race, some of us were walking around Nashville taking in the sights, Jimmy Pardue and some members of our two crews.

This will sound like a disclaimer, but it is a fact. You have heard wild tales of some racers' partying. Not all of us partied in that style. Many of us preferred to go bowling and things like that, this particular group that was strolling Nashville.

Regardless, we always enjoyed a joke.

As we stepped off the curb to cross an intersection, the first car in line at the red light was driven by Jim Paschal, a top race driver, but otherwise more on the quiet side.

David Ethridge, who had by then been assimilated into the group of racers, flipped his left hand out, caught the hood latch on Paschal's car, and up popped the hood.

We kept walking as if nothing had happened, but glanced back.

Paschal was out of his car, putting the hood back in place as motorists to the rear of his car were blowing their horns. Paschal grinned and waggled his finger at us.

Ethridge stayed with our team all that season and the next, until he signed on with one of the tire companies.

You have heard about Cale Yarborough's humor.

A reporter once asked Cale his opinion of David Pearson as a competitor and the reply was, "Well, I'll tell you one thing. He's a hard dog to keep under the porch." Now, that's real country talking.

Some of us were walking through the pit area at Columbia, S.C., prior to a Grand National race, and Bob Welborn, a great driver and former NASCAR Convertible series national champion, was relaxing in the seat of his race car.

One of the fellows moved over to Welborn, "Tell us something funny, Bob."

Welborn grabbed the steering wheel, really tense, looked out the windshield with all seriousness, "Which way did they go?"

HELPING HANDS
NOT APPRECIATED

There are so many vivid memories for so many people, racers and fans, about incidents on the race tracks, but one that will always be remembered by the folks who were sitting in the grandstand that day was the fire which destroyed the stands at Greensboro, N.C.

It was an inferno and the folks scrambled to run for safety.

In those days, fans customarily parked their automobiles very close to the grandstand, the first arrivals, I mean, and the raging flames endangered the automobiles as well as the fans.

The people who were first out of the grandstand began pushing the automobiles to a place of more safety.

Several had hold of one automobile and they were pushing it away from the flames when the irate owner rushed up, "Mind your own business! Leave my car alone!"

He apparently had his thoughts on the insurance settlement he would receive if the car burned.

GATE CRASHING

Two men were standing at one of the gates close to race time, vainly attempting to convince the gate man that they had left their tickets at their motel on the beachside.

With all the heavy traffic, in fact much of it one way from downtown to the speedway, there was no way that they could go to the motel to retrieve the ducats and still see enough of the race.

They told the gate man that they had memorized the seat locations and they quoted row and seat numbers without hesitation.

The man said, "I am truly sorry, but I just cannot let you in without the tickets."

Then a man stepped up and asked the gate keeper, "What's the problem here?"

After the explanations by all hands, he said, "Since they know the row and seat numbers and since it's almost race time, I'll take them up there. If those seats are vacant, then it is apparent they are telling the truth, and they can stay.

"But don't you let anyone else in here no matter what kind of story they tell you, unless I am here. You just turn them away, but do it politely."

"I'll take these two up there, but like I say, don't let anyone else in unless you see me or another speedway official."

"Yes, sir."

The trio went to the top of the hill up to the base of the grandstand and the pair started to turn left, but the well-dressed official turned right.

The two men said, "Hey man, our seats are down this way."

The "official" grinned, "Look, Jack, I don't care where you are sitting. I just wanted to get in here, too."

So, all you gate people, you have to be on your toes. Somebody's always looking to pull a fast one.

There was a fellow in North Carolina who went a bit too far. He had plenty of money, but he just enjoyed the game, the challenge to pull a fast one.

He would walk up to the ticket window with three companions, "Give me four tickets," and hand in a $50 bill. Ticket prices then were about $4 each. As soon as the seller counted the change, the customer would say, "No, give me back the $50 and take it out of this $20." He would hand back the change and get his $50 back.

After he had the ticket seller confused, and of course the correct amount of money and change had been done, he would walk away, and then quickly step back, "Oh, yes, give me the tickets."

The seller would hand over four tickets, forgetting that he had already given out four tickets.

The flim flam artist would hand his friends their tickets, then proceed to sell the extra four to people waiting in line.

And that from a guy who had plenty of money!

One of those incidents happened to me at Kannapolis, N.C., but it was unintentional.

I had some trucks, and one was a furniture moving truck with the canvas on the side, a canvas top and canvas flap on the back. We had rigged a light in the ceiling. When a bunch of us would go to a race, two would ride up front with the driver and the rest would relax in back, playing poker.

This day at Kannapolis, I was driving and my Dad and another fellow were riding with me, a half dozen or so were in the back playing cards.

At the infield gate, I told the man, "Give me three." I wasn't about to pay for the guys in the back.

The gateman asked, "How many do you have in the back?"

"I'll be damned if I know, just count them."

As he started to look in the back of the truck, the other customers behind me were blowing their horns.

The man said, "Oh, hell, I can't hold up these people. Go on through. Get going!"

NIGHT RACING
AND THE FLASHLIGHT

Driving for Cecil Yon at Greenwood, S.C., we had no radios in those days. Especially on a quarter mile track like that, the driver did not have time to read any blackboard messages, so he was usually on his own.

We had hand signals to the pit crews if we were going to stop for tires, gasoline or if the problems were mechanical.

For a longer race one night at Greenwood, Cecil said he would sit on the front row of the grandstand with a flashlight. If all was going well, if I had a good lead, he would aim the flashlight right at my windshield.

If I had to beware of the cars behind me, there would be no signal.

The idea was that we did not want me to be racing somebody hard when there was no need to do so.

Cotton Owens was running good that night, right on my tail, but Cecil thought Cotton was a lap down, so he flipped the light at me.

The next lap around, I saw the flashlight again, so I eased off a bit. There was no need to extend the car if Cotton was no threat.

After the race we discovered that Cotton had been in the same lap, and he had passed me to win, I finished second.

So the best laid plans and so on. This shows how little things, a bit of miscalculation, can be costly.

Darlington, 1950.

SHOWMANSHIP
AND "FIXED" RACES

Historians have recorded that in the earlier days of the 20th century, the post-World War I period, it was not unusual for the drivers to agree on the outcome before the race, so as to put on a better show for the customers.

In later years, it has been alleged that some promoters had their lead drivers under salary contracts, so it made little difference to them who won or lost.

It wasn't an intentional fixed race at Indianapolis when Mauri Rose and Bill Holland were teammates.

Holland, a rookie, was leading the race. Rose was second and car owner Lou Moore said later that he did not want his two drivers racing each other and endanger a one-two finish.

He showed Holland the blackboard with the letters "EZY."

Holland, thinking then he must be a lap ahead of his teammate, followed instructions and let Rose pass.

Only minutes later did he learn the awful truth. they had been in the same lap. Moore always insisted he had no preference which driver won, he just wanted to be sure they finished first and second.

There was a humorous situation at the Richmond, Va., Fairgrounds track they called Strawberry Hill.

Doc Benson's Roaring Roadsters were to race one Saturday night, so the promoters scheduled a match race between a midget and a roadster, just to add to the entertainment.

Al Fleming had his midget, which was obviously faster than any roadster, so he and the roadster driver agreed they would "hippodrome" it, as the phrase went in those days.

For the first few laps, the two put on a show, first the midget would lead, then the roadster, and the crowd was enjoying the show.

On the final lap, Fleming's midget engine quit on the backstretch and the roadster went on to win as the crowd loudly booed.

That was one match race which was an embarrassing disaster. I really shouldn't tell you the promoter's name, because the venture was just a hobby for him at the time.

Max Ailor wrote in the Richmond News-Dispatch the next day, "Last night at Strawberry Hill, Don O'Reilly became an ex-promoter."

I had my own experience with a "hip" race, just once.

At a small South Carolina track one night, Danny Ruff and I had the only good cars there. For some reason, the field was not so hot, perhaps because of a conflicting race elsewhere. The rest of the field was mostly beginners.

The promoter asked us, "I need a good show, so how about you two making it look good, take it easy and don't run away and hide from these other boys. Just put on a show."

Our cars were so superior there would be no contest, so Danny and I agreed. In fact, we went a point further, flipped a coin to determine which of us would win.

We figured if we gave the fans a good show that night, the next time we were there with a good field of cars, the fans would be back and we could run them flat out and belly to the ground.

Danny won the coin toss. We did run a good race, Danny and I swapped the lead, but we were slow enough that the rest of the field was close behind, giving us a good battle, so it seemed.

Suddenly, during the race, a piece of debris went through my car's radiator and I was out.

A short time later, Danny's car became crossed up and he hit the outside wall.

After the race, Danny Ruff and I agreed, "Never again. From now on we will play it like it is supposed to be, give it your best shot regardless."

A NEW KIND OF RACE CAR FUEL

My good friend Pete Keller from Columbia, S.C., has been around racing a long time, as a top car owner, promoter and NASCAR official.

Back in his car-owning days, truckers were beginning to use propane as a fuel, so Keller decided to see if it would improve the performance of his race car.

He had the rig installed and was giving the car its first outing in a race at Columbia.

Something happened during the race, a fitting came loose or whatever and the fumes went into the cockpit, putting the driver to sleep.

Through the fence went the car. The driver was not injured, but the medics administered oxygen and took him to the hospital in the track ambulance.

Later, I asked Keller, "Pete, how much did it cost you to convert your race car over to propane?"

"That isn't the point. It cost me about $150 to put the propane into the car, but it cost me $200 to get it out of my driver.

Not too long ago, Keller and I were emceeing a local track racing banquet and drivers Billy Franklin, Head Hamby and Danny Ruff were there, so I prevailed on Keller to tell that story.

It brought down the house.

ROMANCE AND
THE LOCKED GATE

As I tell you this story about a night at the Columbia, S.C., Speedway, I want to make the point to y'all that this happened *before* I was married.

I became acquainted with a girl who was with her friends in the infield and we talked quite a bit between races, through the fence, she on the infield, me on the track apron area.

It was agreed that we would have a date after the race, so we all met when the race was over. The friends went home and left her in good hands, mine.

We sat in my automobile talking, waiting for the crowd to leave and the traffic to ease, and we were getting acquainted.

We were in no big hurry and it is surprising how two strangers can find so much to talk about.

As we chatted on, the track lights went out, but that was normal because promoters turn the lights out as quickly as they can to save money, but they usually have a lot of work to do before they go home.

After a while, we realized that we were all alone in the infield, and everything was very, very quiet.   I fired up the engine, drove across the track and headed for the gate.

Oops. The gate was locked with a heavy chain and a padlock on the outside.

Taking the jack handle from my car, I climbed over the fence and managed to open the padlock, open the gate, drive through, and then fasten the gate as best I could.

I telephoned the promoter and he was quite understanding. Told me not to worry about it, and I did get the girl home on time.

Some things do go wrong but turn out okay.

RALPH EARNHARDT, FATHER OF THE CHAMPION

When almost everyone was independent, long before the days of the big corporate sponsors, we helped each other.

Dink Widenhouse was a great person and he helped me build a lowboy trailer so I could haul two race cars. He gave me some materials and then he helped with the welding so we could rig an attachment to the fifth wheel of my truck tractor.

After we built it at Dink's place, I hauled everything back home to Charleston, S.C., and finished it. That sure saved a lot of time and expense later. Dink Widenhouse and Bobby Johns were close friends in those days.

Bobby Johns is still living down in the Miami area and he attends several races each year.

Also around the Monroe and Kannapolis, N.C., area then was Bill Widenhouse, who had the nickname of Slab. I never ever figured out how that name came about.

Dink and Bill generally raced the Modified cars. In those days, the Sportsman and the Modified cars ran in the same races, and the promoters paid bonuses to the Sportsman cars because they were obviously slower than the Modifieds.

We Sportsman drivers were limited to one carburetor, the Modifieds were unlimited.

There were many times when a good Sportsman driver could sneak up and win. I won my share, but it wasn't easy.

Ralph Earnhardt and I were racing at Columbia, S.C. He was fifth and I was sixth. No matter how I tried, there was no way I could pass Ralph.

He was just as tough a competitor then as his son is today. The son, I need not tell you, is Dale Earnhardt, reigning NASCAR Winston Cup National Champion and the much acclaimed "One Tough Customer."

Believe me, his daddy was also one tough customer. The race was nearing the end and the field had sort of settled down, running more or less single file, but all at the same speed, and there was no way for Ralph to improve his position or for me to pass him.

Without warning as we entered the backstretch the four cars in the lead were sliding all over the place, banging against each other, almost blocking the track.

We learned later that a sudden rain squall had dumped water on that portion of the race track.

Earnhardt and I had just enough time to avoid the tangle, and we worked our way through, continuing to the finish line where the red flag was out.

The rain continued and the race was never restarted, so Ralph Earnhardt was paid for winning, I was paid for second.

WATCH OUT FOR THAT FIRST STEP!

Neil "Soapy" Castle, car owner Leland Colvin and Bill "Slab" Widenhouse came through my town one day and tried to convince me to go to the West Memphis, Ark., Speedway where they were going to run a well paying race.

I had planned to run a couple short track races close to home and so, for one reason or another, I declined the invitation.

Castle later told me what happened.

Soapy was driving that night when he began to tire, so he told Leland, "I just have to rest a bit. I'm falling asleep."

Colvin said, "Well, reach back there and wake up old Slab. Let him drive a while." You know what they say, rank has its privilege and the car owners were the bosses.

So, Castle reached back and shook Widenhouse and told him to get up and drive for a while. Castle pulled over and stopped by the side of the road, up there in the Tennessee mountains.

Widenhouse rubbed his eyes, opened the door and stepped out in the darkness, straight down. Castle had parked on the very edge of a high banking.

Fortunately, Widenhouse stopped falling when his feet hit a ledge. He was unhurt, but scared, and too far down for Castle and Colvin to reach him.

Passersby heard the screaming and hollering and soon someone had a rope and one way or another, Widenhouse was hauled up to safety, scratched, scraped and mad.

Dink Widenhouse, Kannapolis, N.C.

BEGINNING OF A FRIENDSHIP

I have told you about racing for the Yon Brothers Garage and what a great relationship that was over the years.

Our meeting was quite by chance before a Sportsman race at the Spartanburg, S.C., Fairgrounds, Joe Littlejohn's great little race track.

I didn't have a race car at that time, but I had driven over to the track to see what was going on.

Just inside was a mechanic who was new to me, working on his race car. It was Cecil Yon with his wife Claudia and their children.

When we towed the race cars, which had floating rear ends, we would pull out the axles so the entire drive shaft and transmission drive train would not turn and wear them out, just as today you would never want to tow an automobile with automatic transmission without making disconnects.

On arrival at the destination, it was necessary to put the axles back in place.

That is what Cecil Yon was doing, squatting down and putting in the axles. His children were too young to help, so I introduced myself and offered to help.

He said, "Yeah, okay."

I learned that Doug Cox was his driver but just for that one race, and I told him I was interested if he didn't have a regular driver.

I pitched in and worked with him that day in the pit. I told him where I had raced, against whom I had competed and how I had fared.

He said, "Okay, we'll give it a shot. The next race is at Aiken, S.C. Why don't you just show up there?"

"Okay, suits me fine."

Perhaps we were ahead of our time because of the big dollars today, but the pleasant, casual way of life was nice. I have no regrets and I do have many pleasant memories.

Edison and Cecil Yon, and Eric McKnight, 1951.

TOO MANY FRIENDS
HAD DEPARTED

Along in 1964 when I was running the NASCAR Grand National circuit, the major league of stock car racing, I began to get some strange feelings thinking about the good friends who had died in races, enroute to races or in tire testing, and I began to think, "What am I doing out here to start with?" I would climb in the race car and it just wasn't fun any more, not the way it used to be.

There was the great Fireball Roberts. We used to buddy around a bit after practice, going bowling, getting something to eat.

That terrible day at the Charlotte, N.C., Motor Speedway, there were two cars burning on the race track. As I went by I could see one driver out of the car, and just knew the other driver was still in the car. I couldn't tell who it was. The flames were terrible because there were 42 gallons of fuel flowing on the track from the two cars. That was before we had the fuel cells.

I felt really queasy at that moment. Later, I learned that Roberts had been in the race car and been taken to the hospital where he died of the burns.

Other friends I lost were Little Joe Weatherly, Curtis Turner, Jimmy Pardue, Larry Thomas and Billy Wade.

The last time I saw Billy Wade was at Spartanburg, S.C., after we had tangled and I had demolished my race car.

Wade was out of the race, too, but he was driving for the factory-backed Mercury team and he would have another car for the next race.

I was an independent and it wouldn't be easy putting together another competitive race car.

Billy came to me and said, "Curtis, I am so sorry. I'll do something for you as soon as I can one of these days."

Shortly after that the word came, Billy Wade had died while tire testing. I do have the memory of a good friend.

With so much sad happening in 1964 and some business deals working, I only drove a couple of races in 1965 and I decided it was about time to cut back to some short track racing, or even retire.

When you lose the fun part of anything, you are just not going to do it as well as you can. It is time to think about making changes.

I remember the exhilaration of the beginning of my racing career.

You are sitting in the race car with the best equipment you can come up with. The hopes are high as the cars roll around the track on the pace laps.

A driver, especially a rookie, anticipates the green flag, but butterflies are in the stomach and he is tense, ready to go.

He approaches the flag stand and suddenly the starter will pull back the rolled green flag and signal one more lap.

The driver looks in the mirror to see which idiot tried to jump the gun. It makes him mad. That's the way it was with me the first year.

Then we do get the green flag the butterflies are gone. We are racing! The exhilaration, the excitement, accelerating down the stretch, easing into the corner, coming off the corner you can feel the tires biting. The car is working good and you feel good.

Of course, by the time the race ends whatever was going to happen has happened. You have done well or not so well.

You accept it and then work toward getting ready for the next race, another green flag, another moment of excitement.

CAUGHT IN THE MIDDLE

There is a lot more to being a race driver beyond preparation of the car and the competition on the speedway.

There are many negotiations with sponsors, car owners, car owner backers, speedway promoters and the sanctioning associations. Some times the drivers and crews and car owners are caught in the middle during a contest of power between the racing officials and the corporate leaders on the edges of our sport, and the racers have no voice or control.

My moving away from major league racing in 1965 was in part because of the loss of friends who had passed on, as I mentioned a little while ago.

There was another factor. The 1964 season had been very good for me. I had run 59 of 61 races that season, finished among the top five seven times and 30 times in the top ten. I was sixth in the point standings for the NASCAR Grand National Championship circuit.

It was the best year of my career as an independent, without big corporate backing, and I had acquired the lowboy trailer for hauling the two race cars, a Mercury and a Ford.

Yet, as I said, the fun was going out of it for me, but life does go on.

Especially when there was an offer of a good backer for 1965. The catch was that I would have to switch to Chrysler products and run a Dodge for the '65 season.

The planned deal was that I would be given two Dodge cars, some engines and equipment.

With that in mind, I began to sell off the equipment I had been running in '64. Stick Elliott took the truck-tractor and the lowboy trailer. One of the race cars went to Tennessee and the other to Georgia. As long as I was going to be racing Chrysler products, all the spare parts in inventory went with the race cars.

Then, beyond our control, there was debate between NASCAR officials and the racing divisions of Ford and Chrysler. Chrysler had the hemi engine, so Ford came up with a new engine of its own.

NASCAR officials could see themselves in the middle of a Detroit war and the danger that the word "stock" in stock car racing would have little meaning. There was no way everyone could be happy, no matter what the rules.

Chrysler folks showed their unhappiness with whatever were the new rules and they pulled out of stock car racing for a while. That left King Richard Petty high and dry for a while and the decision hit me like a ton of bricks.

I decided that there was no way that I was going to start all over. I had sold all my equipment. Building back up would have been too tough.

I spent the time around Monks Corner trying to figure which way to turn, and became involved in co-promoting race tracks and doing a lot of flagging around the area.

It was a new field for me, and I enjoyed the change.

GETTING ACQUAINTED
WITH NEW OWNERS

Y ou will recall I told you about a chance meeting with car owner Cecil Yon and his invitation for me to meet him in Aiken, S.C., for a tryout.

Cecil had told his brother Athel that he had met a race driver who would be at Aiken, but he apparently had not given any description of me. Cecil had told me he had a brother named Athel.

When I arrived at Aiken, I went to the pit area and found a man and the Yon Brothers Garage race car. The man was busy getting the car ready, so there was little conversation. I pitched in and started helping him.

I did ask, "Where is Cecil?"

"Well, he couldn't make it today." I figured this must be the brother Athel, so kept on working.

He acted as if I was getting in the way and he kept looking around, up and down the pits. I couldn't figure out what he was looking for. As it turned out, he was looking for me, his driver, but he was expecting a bigger fellow than my 145 pound figure.

Things were not getting any better between us. It seemed that every time he turned around, I was in his way, and I was only trying to help, to make a good impression about my willingness.

It was time for practice and I finally asked, "Mr. Yon, didn't your brother tell you about me meeting you here?"

"Oh, my God. Are *you* Crawfish?"

"Yes, sir. I thought maybe you had figured it out by now."

That was a strange meeting, but we did get things worked out and we had a pretty good race, so Athel was satisfied.

I drove for them for a couple years, up and down the East Coast, and we had a wonderful time.

I was racing the Yon brothers' car in Charlotte one time, and neither Cecil nor Athel was with us. I was in a crash with three or four other cars and the Yons' coupe was badly damaged.

I got some help from a friend who had a spare front axle which fixed it up for towing purposes and we headed for Columbia as quickly as possible.

The crew and I went to Smelgroves' Garage in west Columbia where he had a '37 Ford two-door sedan coach, a popular body style for racing at that time, and which was almost ready to race.

I asked M.C. Smelgrove, "How about selling me that sedan so I can put this man's race car back together?"

Smelgrove used his wrecker truck to help switch the engine and transmission and rear end. Then he used his welder to make the radiator mounts and things like that.

It was a lot of work, but we got the job done, the car ready for racing.

We fired it up and everything was fine.

Both Cecil and Athel and their families planned to meet us at the track in Columbia for the Saturday night race.

We were getting ready for practice when the Yons arrived in the pit area and we leaned up against the race car while we all talked. The car was still its original black because we had not had time to paint it in racing trim.

After a few minutes, the Yons started looking around and Cecil asked, "Where's our race car?"

"Cecil, you're leaning up against it."

We had not had time to tell them about the crash and the change. When the car left their garage it was a coupe. Now they were leaning against a black sedan.

Of course, they were glad that we had taken steps and worked to get the car ready to run and they didn't mind the change.

IT HURTS TOO MUCH TO CRY
SO WE LAUGH

Racing people take their bad lumps as a matter of course and they don't have to like it, but they can chuckle on occasion.

On a short dirt track the engine in my race car exploded on the backstretch and oil was streaming out as I rolled around the track and into the pits.

Pitting next to me at that race was Bob Williams, a good car builder and a fine person.

He looked at the mess I had made and said, "My goodness, Curtis, is that the way you change your oil?"

A few laps later the race was restarted and Bob's driver got his car crossed up on the front stretch, flipping end over end and rolling every which way.

It landed upside down in front of us and the oil was running on the ground. When I saw the driver was unhurt, I asked, "Well, Bob, is that the way you change your oil?"

When racers have mechanical problems of whatever kind, and there is a race the following night, it is routine that everyone pitches in to fix the car, all night if needed.

If we are on the road to the next track, some of the crew can catch a little sleep on the back seat, but the race driver does have to be able to drive the race car that next night.

They often kid, "I didn't have long to sleep last night, so I slept fast."

Buck Baker spoke about adversity: "You may give out, but you don't give up."

THE SILVER FOX

In the early 1950s there was a new young fellow starting as a race driver and he had the usual problems of most newcomers, keeping his car on the race track, learning the ropes.

But this fellow came on pretty doggone fast.

The newcomer, David Pearson, was destined to be a three-time Grand National Champion and the second biggest race winner in NASCAR G.N. with 105 victories.

When I first saw him as a newcomer he had a fastback sedan, as they called it, racing around Spartanburg, Greenville and Columbia, S.C., and he was the man to beat with that good looking race car.

He began his Grand National racing in 1960 and won Rookie of the Year honors.

The following year Pearson showed up at the Charlotte Motor Speedway to drive a Pontiac for the prestigious builder Ray Fox. At first, some people wondered why Fox had chosen a rookie, but after Pearson and Fox had won the World 600, Fox looked like a genius and Pearson gained respect.

Pearson established himself as a top NASCAR driver in 1961 when he added the Daytona Firecracker 400 and the Atlanta International Raceway Dixie 400 to his victory skein.

If ever a man is destined for the Hall of Fame, it is David Pearson, the Silver Fox, race driver, husband and father, businessman and all round nice guy.

Another person who made a good and lasting impression

David Pearson and "Corky".

on me is Sam McQuagg.

The crew and I were sitting around in a motel room in Georgia one evening, making plans for the race the next day.

A young fellow stuck his head in the open doorway and said, "Hi, folks. I'm Sam McQuagg."

He had not run any Grand National races to that time so he made it a point to meet all of us. He was great. He got some good Grand National rides, but he did not stay with it too many years because he insisted on racing only in top notch equipment, which was not always available. He had been a frequent winner on the NASCAR Sportsman circuit.

After one short track Grand National race in 1962, McQuagg returned to Grand National in 1964 and his first race was the Daytona Beach Firecracker 400. He ran five races in 1964, then embarked on the Grand National career in 1965, winning Rookie of the Year honors and in 1966 he won the Firecracker 400.

It is unique how some people can suddenly appear on the scene with great natural ability and make their mark so quickly.

Others can race all their lives and don't realize that they are not really cut out for it.

An outstanding feature about Sam McQuagg was that he was, and probably still is, an outstanding pilot with his own airplane. We miss that 49-year-old from Columbus, Ga.

There are many of you folks out there, guys and ladies both, who have been wishing to get involved in racing. If you feel like doing it and think you can do it and are willing to put in the time and effort, go ahead and do the best you can.

You will probably have to start on some short track with the hobby type equipment and the more experience you gain and the longer you stay with it, you will move up in class.

If you find that you have that natural talent and gain a little bit of an edge, you will be a front-runner.

It's fine to be aggressive and a hard charger, but be considerate of other contestants, intentional bammin' and frammin' does not work. You are more apt to get banged back, doubled.

If you do give it a try and then find that after a season or so you don't have that knack or can not get the financial wherewithal, it is my suggestion that you hang it up before you hurt yourself or someone else. You gave it the good try.

Look around and see if some other phase of the sport may be more your style - mechanic, flagman, technical inspector, speedway office worker, whatever.

This is a great sport and a great business and there are many jobs to be done, many openings from time to time.

Good luck and God bless!

Hershel McGriff at First Darlington 500 Race, in 1950. NASCAR Point Champion Winston West, 1986.

A MEMORY OF NORRIS FRIEL

For the Atlanta International Raceway in 1963, I had ordered a brand new Mercury which came with a 427 cubic inch displacement engine.

During the blueprinting and rebuilding of the engine, getting it ready to race, I discovered that the valves and heads were a bit smaller than normal.

There was a four-barrel intake and everything else seemed okay, but the head that had been assembled at the factory had valves that were slightly smaller than expected. Not much, but still a difference.

I was well familiar with the NASCAR rules that you can't bore the cylinders too much and you can't have items larger than normal, but I wasn't worried about smaller valves.

The next race was at Nashville and there wasn't sufficient time to go to Charlotte and pick up another set of cylinder heads.

There didn't seem to be enough difference to cause a problem and later I could contact the factory people and find out what was the problem, and get it fixed.

We raced Nashville with no problems and headed to Atlanta for the 500-mile race coming up.

My wife was in the hospital in Charleston, S.C., so I left the boys in Atlanta and drove straight through to the hospital.

When I returned to the Atlanta International Raceway, I found the car in the inspection area and the engine had not been put back together, and it was covered up.

The boys explained that they had pulled the engine down for inspection and the officials said the valves were too small. NASCAR had confiscated the heads.

I went straight to the trailer where Norris Friel, the head inspector, had his office. "Norris, what in the world has happened?"

"The valves are too small and you had the wrong heads on the engine."

"My God, Norris. I'm not cheating or anything. You know that. They're not too big. I don't understand that."

Norris said, "It works the other way, too. If you run smaller valves, you get better gas mileage. There is only one set of valves that you should run. I have no choice."

I had to agree that he had a good point. Here I was with a new race car and no cylinder heads. My wife was in the hospital and I needed the money. I needed to run in that race and earn some money.

Then something happened that hadn't occurred in many years, nor even since. I broke down.

I climbed up into the seat of my truck, which was sitting there facing toward the infield. I had just given out from running back and forth to Charleston to visit my wife in the hospital, getting the new car ready, going to Nashville to race and back to Atlanta.

I needed to race, to work, to earn money for the hospital bills and to pay my crew.

I sat there in the truck and cried like a baby until I got it out of my system.

Then I got out of the truck, calmed down, got into the pickup truck and drove to Atlanta to the Mercury dealer.

I asked if they had the heads and valves that I needed. They did, and they recognized my name as one of the regular Mercury race drivers, so I got the parts.

I then asked if I could use their machine shop to work on the heads and they let me do that.

I knew I didn't have to worry about the ccs, because the 427 engines were usually right on the money in that area, meeting the NASCAR specifications.

The real problem was getting the right valves and getting the engine back together for the race.

We used the machine shop equipment, put the heads back

together, loaded them in the pickup truck and headed for the raceway.

I had the cylinder heads and valves inspected, and they passed, so I gave them to the boys and said, "Now, let's go racing."

Later, during a practice session, a man from the Mercury dealership came out to the raceway and he came up to us while we were standing on pit road waiting for them to open the gate for practice.

He handed me a bill for the cylinder heads and the valves.

Up against the pit wall a few feet away was Fran Hernandez, Mercury Division's racing activities man from Detroit.

I said to the dealership man, "C'mon up here. There is someone I want you to meet."

I introduced the two of them and told the man from Atlanta, "This is the man you want to talk to, right here. I ordered a new car from the factory with the right kind of engine. It was delivered with the wrong cylinder heads and wrong valves.

"Now, Norris Friel over there at NASCAR has your set of heads, Mr. Hernandez, and I have mine sitting in the race car here on pit row.

"Now you two get together and see what y'all can do about this thing."

I just walked away.

I had not had a chance to let the Mercury people know about their error. I was going to take care of that after Atlanta.

I never heard another word about it from anyone, not even Fran Hernandez.

My car was in good shape, I guess the factory folks paid the dealer. I do know that Norris Friel had my so-called illegal cylinder heads and he sent them someplace to put on display as they do with other "cheating" equipment.

Al Jenkins, Pete DePaolo, Cannonball Baker, 1956

RACERS CARE,
BEHIND THE SCENES

The 1963 Atlanta 500 week was a troublesome one, with all the problems about the cylinder heads and my running back and forth to the hospital in Charleston, S.C., but there was a totally unexpected incident which I will never forget.

The car was about ready to race, those troubles were behind me and the crew, when a NASCAR official came by and said they were taking up a collection for somebody who really needed it. No names were mentioned.

We had had so much expense, car and hospital, that I was pretty low in that department. "Well, I don't have much on me, but I'll give you what I can."

"That will be fine, Curtis. That's all we ask."

I counted the money, figured how much I would need to feed the crew that Saturday night and for Sunday Breakfast, and said, "I'll give you half of what I have." I figured that was being fair.

The man thanked me and they went through the garage area collecting from everybody.

Sunday morning, race day, at the drivers' meeting, one of the NASCAR men said he had an announcement to make.

They presented to me the collection they had taken for Mary Frances and me because of our hospital expense.

After all the trouble about the cylinder heads, the Atlanta Mercury dealer, my sobbing while sitting in the truck, this was so unbelievable, so touching, so emotional. It really got to me.

They had a list of the guys who had donated, Cotton Owens, the Wood brothers, the Bakers, Ray Fox and crew, Bobby Johns and Papa Johns and crew, so many of them, all down the line, the car owners, officials and some of the sports writers. Yes, my name was on the list, too.

A man never forgets and it makes one realize how auto racing is really a family, especially stock car racing. They may fuss and argue and do battle on the race track, but when someone needs help, they are there, even without being asked.

THE WORLD'S SKIMPIEST
PIT CREW

Atlanta International Raceway was no better or worse for me than any other track, except when it rained. You will remember that the Atlanta Journal sports editor once nicknamed the place "Atlanta International Rainway."

We were back the following spring for the 1964 Atlanta 400 and I had two race cars then. Frank Graham, out of Charleston, S.C., was my other driver.

Everything seemed set to run a pretty good race with both cars. We had qualified well, the cars seemed right. It was a better period than 1963.

Then it rained, and the race was postponed. A.I.R. seemed to be jinxed back then, for several years, with more rainouts or rain delays than any other track around.

So, all the crews went home to race another day. The race cars were impounded by NASCAR, as is customary with postponements.

Come race day, Frank and I were there, our race cars were on pit row and one of our men was there, Warren Prout from Charleston.

Something had happened to the rest of the crew, enroute from Charleston to Atlanta.

Prout said he felt awful small and out of place, standing in that seemingly huge pit with two race cars, while up and down the wall were five or six men for every other car.

"Well, all you can do," I told Warren, "is hope that the guys do come through that tunnel. If they don't, try and get some help perhaps from some team whose car has dropped out of the race. Just do the best you can. When the green flag drops, Frank and I have to do our own thing out on the track."

Warren told me later that he was sorely tempted to take off right then, but he did stick around, he did borrow some willing hands and both Frank and I finished the race with fairly decent pit stops.

There were many interesting things like that which were happening during racing times 20 and 30 years ago, little things that escaped the notice of the fans in the grandstands and even the auto racing sports writers at times.

A speedway is a big place, there is much doing in the garage area and the pits, and the drivers do not publicly complain about their problems, just make the best of it.

Ed Livingston, Curtis Crider and able help.

YOU MEET THE NICEST PEOPLE

After I had been racing out of Columbia, S.C., for a couple of years, among my friends was Ed Livingston, a fun-loving fellow who had brothers who were mechanically inclined.

They decided that I seemed to be enjoying myself and knew how to get to the race tracks and what to do, so he decided to run a Grand National car himself. He is one of the few who started directly in Grand National cars in those days.

Richard Petty is about the only one I know who did that in that era.

When someone painted the driver's name on the edge of the roof of Ed's race car, he painted the words "*DR.* Ed Livingston" instead of the usual "Ed Livingston, Driver."

It didn't register with me, but other folks immediately had the impression that the new driver was a doctor.

Ed loved a joke, so he went along with it when he was asked about his profession.

"Oh, yes. I'm a vet. I'm an S.M.D."

"What's an S.M.D.?"

"See More Dogs."

Ed did quite well. In fact, he had a third place finish in a race in Jacksonville, and that was pretty good for a newcomer.

He got along good with all the guys. Everyone liked Ed.

Francis Hudgins.

CALM DOWN, FELLOWS, COOL IT

The night before one of the races at the Atlanta International Raceway, the crew and I were in our motel, which was located between Jonesboro and Atlanta, a few miles north of the Raceway.

We were joined by another driver and his crew, U.S. Air Force Sgt. Roy Tyner, who raced as frequently as his military duties would permit.

They had been in a small town south of the raceway and something happened that got them involved in a brawl. It looked to me that some of the Tyner crew had got the worst of the deal.

Tyner said that he and his friends did not like the idea that they had been jumped upon and the more they talked about it in our motel room, the angrier they got.

Tyner was ready to recruit some help and go back down there and have it out with the people who had jumped them. There was no other way about it, they were going down to look for the locals.

I finally agreed, "Okay, let's go look for them. You say this happened around Hampton? Well, let's look for them in Atlanta."

"Atlanta?!? They won't be there!"

"I know. That's the general idea. We'll go up to Atlanta and look for them. We'll look all night with you if you want."

By that time, Tyner could see that I was making some

sense. If you see a friend being beaten up, you pitch in and help, but after it is all over, you just don't go back looking for the antagonist and start it up all over again.

Roy and his crew got themselves cleaned up, got something to eat and turned in for the night.

So did my crew and the next morning we were all fresh, ready for racing. After all, that is what we came to Atlanta to do.

As Kenny Rogers sings, you have to know when to hold them and when to fold them.

A BEARD AND A VICTORY

Along time friend of the family, Johnny Handy out of Greensboro, N.C., was pitting for me for a while when I was running the Grand National Championship circuit and I wasn't having any success in getting that first victory.

Johnny had announced that he wasn't going to shave again until I won a race.

I warned him that he might be tripping over his beard one day and would regret that vow. He insisted he would stick with it.

The next race after that was at the very tight Bowman Gray Stadium in Winston-Salem, N.C.

The schedule there always called for a pair of 25-lap qualifying races before the feature.

I was the winner of one of those heat races, from start to finish, with Richard Petty second and Fred Lorenzen third.

I was excited. My first Grand National victory!

Then I made a spur of the moment decision, one that a big winner would not have done, but a first time winner could get away with it.

I drove the car around the track and stopped at the flagman's stand, climbed out and jumped over the guard rail as he tried to guess what the heck I was going to do.

I motioned for the checkered flag in his hand, so he handed it to me.

I climbed back into the race car, then circled the track with the flag sticking out the window like the short track Modified and Sportsman drivers do at their weekly races.

The crowd went wild when they realized this was my first victory in a Grand National car.

Yes, Johnny Handy was able to shave that night, even though the beard had only grown to a stubble.

From Left: Tim Flock, Speedy Thompson, Fonty Flock, Carl Keikeifer at Hillsboro Speedway (about 1956).

SOME WILD N' CRAZY HAPPENINGS

In the old days, there were some great drivers racing around the Winston-Salem, N.C., area, men such as Glen Wood, Shorty York, Bobby and Billy Myers and Ted Swain. So many more, just a whole bunch who ran the short tracks, dirt and asphalt.

The half-mile dirt track at High Point, N.C., had a little guard rail made from two inch by ten inch boards, just enough to slow down a car a bit, and there was a big board fence about six and eight feet high designed mainly to keep the non-paying customers from looking in.

One time a driver went through the guard rail at the edge of the track and the car continued down to the high wooden fence. The car struck the fence right between two upright posts and as the entire section of fence came down in one piece the race car kept right on rolling.

The driver was okay, so it was decided they wouldn't delay the race. Instead, they would get the race car after the race was over.

After the race, some of us left the pit area to go back and lend a hand getting the car back to the track.

As we reached the area, we heard some moans and there were two guys on the ground under that fence.

It seems they were peeping through the knot holes in the fence when the race car hit it.

Fortunately, the ground there was very soft dirt, so when

they were flattened under the fence, they were not injured more than some bruises and, of course, scared half to death from being trapped there so long. Actually, because of the uneven ground surface, the fence more or less formed a bridge over them. It was a miracle they were not killed.

I'll bet that's the last time they were freeloaders.

Another time at that same track, it was quite dusty when they started the race, but because there had only been two or three cars on the track at one time in practice, folks had no idea how bad it really was.

All the cars made the first lap of the race okay, but on the second lap something happened to the leading car and instead of turning left at the turn, it went straight out through the fence and four more cars, the drivers blinded by dust, followed that lead car right out of the track.

The worst part of that bargain was that there were huge boulders outside the track and all the cars were badly torn up after hitting the rocks.

At Draper Speedway, a couple of freeloading race fans were watching from high up in a tree outside the track.

A car got out of control, went outside the race track and knocked down the old tree, with the two men still in it.

The race was stopped while the spectators were loaded into the ambulance for the trip to the hospital. They were not injured too badly, but I guess it taught them a lesson, too.

Ken Rush (#94), at High Point, N.C. Whoops!

FIRST VISIT TO SAVANNAH

Among the fine drivers who came out of central Georgia in the late '50s and early '60s were Jack Smith, now operating a chain of automotive transmission shops, and Nero Steptoe and Gober Sosebee.

Steptoe and Sosebee were in the field the day I first visited the track at Savannah, Ga.

The track was banked quite high on the outside of the turn, and the entrance to the pit area inside the race track was across the track between the third and fourth turns.

As the track was fairly high banked, that edge of the track was much higher than the access road. We had to tow our race cars up a grade and over the top of the bank, then down the track to the infield. No great problem, usually.

When we arrived at the track, we drove halfway around the outside of the turn to get ready to cross the track, and I could hear some cars practicing, so we waited for the all clear.

Suddenly one of the cars lost a wheel in the third turn and out came the race car, right through the guard rail, like an arrow right across in front of us.

I wondered aloud, "Oh my, what kind of a track have I gotten myself into here?"

Actually, it was a better looking place once we got inside. The normal racing view was great and I always enjoyed racing in Savannah, even though I never met Hard Hearted Hannah, the vamp of Savannah.

I was running a '40 Ford in a Sportsman race at Savannah

when the officials had to red flag the field because of a wreck in the number two turn.

There were only a few laps to go and the track was not dusty, but they decided to put out the water truck anyway, needed or not.

During the stop, a man came out of the infield and walked up to the car and just wanted to talk. He noticed I was not wearing gloves and asked, "Do you want to wear my gloves?"

Actually I didn't like to wear gloves but I didn't want to hurt his feelings so I accepted. A half dozen laps couldn't hurt me.

At the restart, Larry Flynn's car was in front of mine. We made one lap around the track to get ready for the green, and it was quite wet.

As we came off the fourth turn and got the green flag, Larry got down on the accelerator pedal and he threw two rooster tails of mud right over the front of my car and "turned out my lights."

The '40 Ford had a two piece windshield and we always removed the right side, passenger side, glass anyway. I couldn't see a thing out of the left side glass and couldn't get my foot up high enough to kick out the glass.

I remembered I was wearing the man's gloves, reached forward and punched out the windshield. It slipped right over the top of the car. I don't know what the guy in back of me thought.

I could see really good and I ran Larry Flynn down and won the race, something I couldn't have done without the stranger's offer of the loan of his gloves.

Another time when I was racing the Yon Brothers' Garage car at Savannah, we arrived late at the track and officials wouldn't let us time trial for a starting position. We would have to start in the rear.

That didn't bother me much, but it got on Cecil Yon's nerves. He didn't like it one bit.

That day, David Ezell and some other good drivers from Jacksonville were in the race, so there was an extra bit of rivalry.

Cecil was so upset that he told the officials, "Well, I'll tell you what we are going to do. As soon as this race is over, we want to run against whoever wins it in a match race, winner take all."

When they made that announcement, the crowd got excited.

We ran the race, with me starting last. David Ezell won the race and I was third.

Almost all the fans remained in the grandstand waiting for the match race between Ezell and me.

Cecil and I put up what money we had won and a little more, and Ezell put up an equal share.

I had told Cecil that during the feature race I had lost my brakes. After I had worked up to third place, I had to ease off some, and held the position, but couldn't gain.

"No problem," he said.

Cecil worked on the brakes and told me it was all okay, now.

What I didn't know was that he had found a broken brake line to the rear wheels, and hadn't had enough time to repair it.

He beat the rear brake lines together with a hammer so they wouldn't leak, then filled up with brake fluid so I had front brakes only. He didn't tell me that.

I drew to start on the inside pole position, David on the outside.

With the green flag, I pulled ahead about a car length and going down the backstretch I was gaining all the time. I went into the third turn as hard as I had ever been there, and decided it was time to tap the brakes.

That turkey just shot straight up toward the wall. I eased off the brake and got back on the gas and worked the car through the turn.

Naturally, David went under me and he was flying down the front stretch.

I could catch him but I couldn't do a damn thing with him.

Every time I touched the brake pedal, the car would go straight to the outside wall.

Needless to say, David Ezell won the race and all our money.

That taught us a lesson then and there.

Pete Folse, Hector Honore (L) and Gene Van Winkle (R). Pete ran sprint cars after he returned from England.

SKINNY TIRES
AND SMALL SPINDLES

In the early days at the Darlington, S.C., Raceway, the tires were really too skinny for that kind of racing and the spindles were small, so handling in the corners was at a premium.

Jack Smith's car was out of control one day in the first turn and he went over the guard rail and out.

Of course, his car was not the only one to do that. You've heard of Cale Yarborough's wild ride. There were others.

It has been said that Jack once commented that every time he would go down the front straightaway after that, his right foot would automatically raise up.

The tires were not really good, they were what amounted to truck tires of that day.

The most awful sound at any speedway, whether you were in a race car or a grandstand, was the big boom of a tire blowing out, which sounded like a cannon.

When a fellow like me was working on the car, trying to get the right weight distribution, fellows like Fred Lorenzen, Nelson Stacy, Ralph Moody or Fireball Roberts would walk by.

If you looked like you were ready to scratch your head in wonderment, they would jump up and down on the springs and say, "Well, go a little heavier" or "Go a little lighter." They did help a lot.

Ralph Moody was a former race driver before he was a car builder, and he was one of the best at both jobs.

When Moody would bring a car to the raceway, he would take it out on the track first and test it, make changes to make it handle better.

Then he would tell his driver to get in.

Moody knew what the car was capable of doing, and it was up to the driver to practice a bit more and reach the same goal.

Skinny Tires: Kinda Scary.

THE POPULARITY VOTE

Augusta, Ga., is the famous home of the Masters golf tournament, but little known is that it was also host to NASCAR Grand National stock car racing for a short period of time.

Some folks had built a beautiful speedway, but for whatever reason it did not remain operational for very many years.

Officials decided to hold an impromptu popularity contest, each driver voting for his favorite driver, and they passed out paper ballots.

We were instructed to write any driver's name, our own name if we wanted.

When I was leaning against Richard Petty's race car talking to his father, Lee Petty, I had the ballot in my hand.

Lee asked, "Who did you vote for?"

"I voted for Tiny Lund. He just started running with us and I figured he needed a vote or two to lift his spirits."

Lee continued, "Well, Richard just started, too, not too long ago. why don't you vote for Richard?"

I liked Richard. Tiny Lund's name had just come to mind when they handed me the ballot, so I thought about a minute and said, "Okay, I'll vote for Richard." They were both deserving.

I changed the ballot and turned it in.

When the race officials counted the ballots, they discovered that they had a tie for the winner. They also noted they were short one ballot. One driver had not voted.

Checking around they learned that Wendell Scott was the one who had not voted. He had been busy working on his race car. They sent a messenger to Wendell with a ballot, and he hastily scribbled the name of Richard Petty.

Then it was announced the tie had been between Richard Petty and Curtis Crider, and Wendell Scott's vote gave the title and the trophy to Richard.

I had no regrets. I was proud that the fellows thought enough of me to give me that many votes. I feel honored to have run second to Richard Petty any time. Ned Jarrett won the race, Richard Petty was second and I was third - just behind Petty again.

Today, NASCAR's Most Popular Driver contest is on a well organized basis, nationwide, conducted by the National Motorsport Press Association.

Awesome Bill Elliott was recently proclaimed the winner, the most popular driver for the second year in a row.

WENDELL SCOTT
A NASCAR LEGEND

I first met Wendell Scott when he was racing around the Winston-Salem, N.C., area and we became good friends. We had something in common, we were both born in Danville, Va. My folks and I had moved away when I was a boy, but Wendell had stayed.

In fact, Wendell Scott continues to operate a garage in Danville as you read this.

Wendell always held his own on the race tracks in the Sportsman racing days and did his own work on the race cars, just as I did. It was the same when he moved up into Grand National racing.

Undoubtedly there were some special problems being a black person in the sport, but there was no animosity among the drivers and the crews.

Wendell was an independent just as were a lot of us, and he didn't have much money, just like a lot of us.

In those days, race teams would help each other, lending tools, tires, even entire engines. There are many cases on record when one driver would lend equipment to a competitor and then the competitor would win the race.

If Wendell needed help, someone would help him. If I needed something and Wendell had it, he would lend it to me.

At every race, you would find me and others visiting with Wendell in the garage area and in his pit on practice days.

Herman Beam, LeLand Colvin, John Brunner, Wendell Scott, 1963.

When we would all go to California for the two Riverside International Raceway Grand National races each year, it was a financial strain on all the independents, some more than others.

In those earlier days of racing at Riverside, a lot of people did not have truck haulers to transport their race cars and it was a long trip, often times a lonely trip, but we did keep in touch with each others' whereabouts to a degree.

Some of us had left the Carolinas and Virginia a bit earlier than had Scott and enroute we had heard reports that he was in Texas and then in Arizona. Most of us were at the Raceway, but no Scott car. The word was that he was getting closer.

The NASCAR rule at Riverside was that all cars had to be checked in by 4 p.m. Thursday. They did have to have some rules of order, otherwise they would never get practice and qualification completed.

With Wendell still among the missing, many of us were getting concerned, thinking about him while we worked on our own cars. Stock car racing is really a family situation. We are all members of the family. Sometimes we quarreled, but otherwise we stuck together.

It was Thursday noon. Then half the afternoon had passed and still no Wendell Scott. Finally came the announcement, "Okay, fellows. Get your tools picked up and boxed up, shut up and get out of here. That's it for today."

Just as some of us were walking toward the road away from the garage, here came Wendell and his race car, just barely in the nick of time. There were not even seconds to spare when he got the nose of his tow car through the gate. Then his car stalled.

There were about 30 of us who reached the gate at the same time. His tow car was steaming, which was why he was late. He had had to baby the thing on the highway because of a heating problem.

Those 30 pairs of hands grabbed that tow car and the race car and pushed them inside the gate so Wendell would be considered as checking in under the deadline. The officials went along with it. No one wanted to see Wendell make that trip all the way across the country for naught.

Wendell did race and he had a good finish and made some money that weekend at Riverside, Calif.

Herman and Wendell plot race strategy.

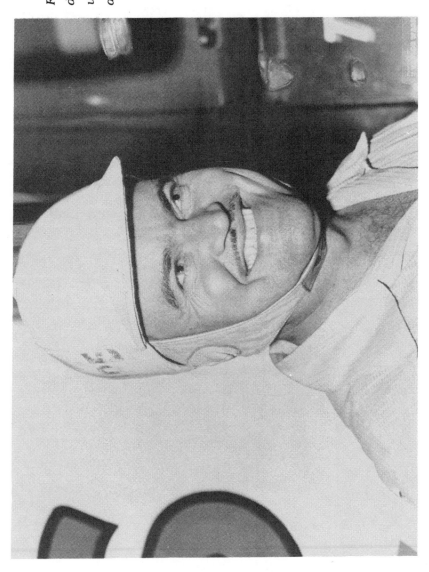

Fonty Flock, in the days when a polo cap was considered adequate protection.

THE MISSING TROPHIES
AND THE RECOVERY

In 1973 when I had the paving business and lived in Ormond Beach, I raced regularly at the Volusia County Speedway in Barberville, just a few miles west of Ormond Beach on the road to Ocala.

That is a neat half-mile dirt oval, very popular on Saturday nights. There have been many times when I was not driving a race car there so I would be the track flagman.

This particular Saturday night, my wife and daughter had left the speedway a little early.

I was still packing my equipment away and getting the car on the hauler to go home when my wife telephoned me at the track to say there had been a burglary at our home.

I told her to call the Sheriff's Department. I left most of the crew at the track to pack the racing equipment and I drove to my house with Don Brooks, one of the crew members.

After a complete examination, we could see that the burglars had taken nothing but my trophies, in fact had selected the best ones, the championship trophies.

It was strange that nothing else in the house had been touched.

I had won the Florida State Championship three years in a row and had a lot of track championships from around Central Florida. The police had already arrived by the time I got home and they made a complete report and took a list and description of all the trophies.

The more I thought about it, I decided that there was one prime suspect. The police said they couldn't go and search someone's house just based on my suspicion. They needed more evidence, at least a witness who might have seen him around my house during the time when the burglary might have occurred.

They did take his name and address from me and said they would check him out, but they would need hard evidence, such as if someone saw him with one of my trophies.

The man who I had in mind had been in the Daytona Beach area only a short time and he claimed to be the brother of a well known racing driver. I had my doubts about this fellow, but not having anything concrete, I and others had accepted him as who he said he was.

The man said he was Johnny Yarborough, brother of Cale Yarborough. Now, Cale was a good friend of mine. In fact, Cale and I had raced together, but I had not seen Cale's brother, J.C. Yarborough since J.C. was a kid, back on the farm near Timmonsville.

"Johnny" said he was staying at one of the major beachside motels in Daytona Beach and he wanted me to build a race car for him or sell him one of mine. The man who called himself J.C. or Johnny said he was going to start a short track team.

We did talk for several days and he did seem to have all the answers and information about Cale, all the general information that I would know, but I never did get enough involved to really want to check him out.

One day he came down into the lobby of that nice motel and screamed that he had been robbed. His room had been broken into and all his money and credit cards and driver's license were gone, picked clean.

The motel manager felt sorry for him and said they would put him up for a few days and they helped him a bit until he could get organized.

Well, I began to smell a rat, as they say, because I would have expected J.C. Yarborough to telephone Cale about being robbed. Knowing Cale, he would have probably got in his airplane there in Florence, S.C., and would have flown to

Daytona Beach right away, or would have at least telegraphed the needed money to his brother.

This went on for days and he had worn out his welcome at the motel; they evicted him.

I figured right away it was this turkey who had stolen my trophies. I talked with Don Brooks, who was a former policeman, and I said, "Look, the police can't do a lot about getting the trophies back, but we can. We have a little more freedom. They have restrictions. Let's go across the river and I know somebody who might tell us where Mr. Yarborough is."

That someone was the caretaker of the motel, who had been hanging around with the alleged J.C.

By then it was two o'clock Sunday morning, but we got him out of bed. He went out to the car with me where I had assembled a couple more guys from my pit crew. We had a big old Mercury four-door sedan and it looked like a squad car.

With one of the crew driving the Mercury, we shoved the motel caretaker into the back seat, between me and another crew member.

"We have a little problem with Johnny and you are supposed to be his best friend. I want you to tell me where you think he might be. You're going to ride around with us tonight and show us where all his girlfriends live.

"We are going to every place until we find him or find the car he is driving. If you don't help us, you are going to be in trouble, too. Now, let's start riding."

"Yes, sir. I'll help you any way I can."

I knew where some of Johnny's friends lived, but I let this guy lead us to all the houses and motels. We went from one place to another and finally, at a motel in South Daytona, we spotted the car he had borrowed.

I called the police from a pay phone, but they said they still could not search his room without proof. They had to see one of the trophies, something like that.

I was going to wait there until he came out of that motel, and I figured it wouldn't be until the next morning, so I sent the other guys home. No need for them to stay up all night for nothing.

Don Brooks drove them home and then came back to join me. We waited there all night on the stakeout as you see in the television detective shows.

About ten in the morning a girl came out of the motel room and I recognized her. She worked in a bar which opened at 11 a.m.

I gave her time to get to work, then telephoned her at the bar and asked, "Where's Johnny? He was supposed to come to my house last night and pick up some of his trophies."

"Well, he did go somewhere and he got a bunch of them. Maybe he didn't get by your house to get the ones he had left there."

"Well, he must not have because I didn't see him."

I knew then that I had him pegged. He was the one who had stolen my trophies.

Expecting that he had another dude in the motel room, one who was supposed to be a pretty big, tough guy, I figured we would need some backup help, so I called a friend who had a trucking business in Ormond Beach, Fred Leo, and told him my problem and asked him to come to the motel with his two sons.

Don Brooks had gone to the coffee shop to get us some food when here came Johnny out of the motel room, headed for the telephone booth.

I walked up to him, met him in the middle of the street, on the median, and he was surprised. We walked over behind the telephone booth and into the bushes.

When we came out from behind the phone booth, Johnny was ready to tell me where my trophies were.

About that time, Fred Leo and his two boys arrived and he had two other truckers with him. Believe me, they even scared me.

"Is this the one that got your stuff, Mr. Curtis?"

"Yeah, this is the one and we're going to get the stuff back."

One of them said, "Well, let's just take him down to the lighthouse and he ain't coming back."

I said, "No, we can't do that. Let's get my stuff first and then we'll decide what we are going to do with Mr. Johnny Yarborough or whoever he is."

We put him in the back seat of the big old Mercury between the two burly truck drivers. They had been out partying and drinking the night before and they smelled as bad as they

— 180 —

looked. They were really mean looking and they were in a mean, surly mood as well.

I was driving with Fred Leo up front, and Don Brooks was to drive Fred's car back and follow us.

Johnny had told me, over there in the bushes, that after stealing my trophies he had gone to bars all over Daytona Beach.

He had a racing suit and helmet under his arm and he would tell the bartender that he had just won that trophy and he was going to give it to the bar. Then everybody in the place would buy him drinks, and he would go on to the next bar and pull the deal all over again.

I told him, "Now, I know how many trophies are missing. Don't you try to pull anything on me, buddy. You just take us to where those trophies are."

We rode all over town that afternoon, picking up trophies.

I would push him in front of me into the bar, holding him by the back of the collar, and walk straight to the bartender.

"Okay, give me my trophy. This is the s.o.b. who stole it from my house last night."

Invariably they would all hand the trophies over and apologize. They were just so sorry about it and were mad for having been taken in by the phony.

"That's quite all right. We've got it straightened out." Out the door we would go and drive to the next bar and the next bar and so on.

At the last bar, on the Mainland side of the Daytona Beach-Holly Hill area, a friend of mine and fellow race car driver, Gordon Cheesbro, who is also a well known businessman in the area, was talking with the bartender. Gordon's back was to the door and he did not see us walk in.

He said, "Now, listen. I'm going to tell you like I told you last night, that guy did not win that trophy. That's Curtis Crider's trophy. I was there when he won that race and I know it is his trophy."

I spoke up, "Does anybody in here know this s.o.b.? He's the one who broke into my house and stole my trophies last night."

Gordon jumped up and shouted, "Yeah, I told you about that last night."

The man who ran the place was hopping mad. He threw down his eye glasses and he was coming around the bar to get a piece of that Johnny.

I said, "No, it's all right. Just give me my trophy and everything will be all right."

He was mad because he had believed the guy and here Gordon had been arguing with him about it.

A man was sitting there in the bar and he spoke up, "Curtis, if you will wait a few minutes, I'll go home. This guy gave me another trophy last night to give to my little boy who's partially crippled. I'll go home and get it and bring it back."

That shook me, so I said, "Well, I'll tell you what we will do. You go to your house and talk to your little boy. Tell him that this trophy means a lot to me and if he will let me have it back we will take care of that situation.

"Y'all come out to the Volusia County Speedway next Saturday night and I'll get him a trophy as close as possible to this one and personally present it to him. But each one of the trophies I have won in races means a lot to me personally."

He went home and brought the trophy back.

The next Saturday night we met at the speedway and I bought a trophy and presented the boy with his very own trophy.

After that session in the last bar, we still had the problem of what to do with the alleged Johnny.

We went to the parking lot and I told this Johnny, "Let me tell you something. You just blew into town here. This is my town. You don't have any more business here whatsoever.

"Everyone in town now, all the bars, they know what kind of a four-flusher you are and you can't show your face around.

"There are two ways you can go. We can take you to the Interstate and you can start hitchhiking in any direction you want, except into the Daytona Beach area. Or I can let these guys take you down to the lighthouse, but it is doubtful you will be able to go in any direction."

He was crying and all shook up. He couldn't understand how I had caught up with him so quickly and how it had all blown up in his face so bad. He decided he would rather go to the Interstate. I told him he couldn't take anything, just the clothes he had on, because I had wasted a full night and day and I wasn't about to drive him all over town to get his things.

"I'm going to tell you something. Don't even think about coming back into town, because if you do some of these people will let me know about it. They'll all be looking for you. We won't take you to the Interstate the next time."

We dropped him off at an I-95 interchange.

About ten o'clock that night he telephoned me at home, "Could I please have a little more time to come and get my stuff together?"

"Take all the time you want, buddy, but don't let anyone see you. The first one that sees you will call me and it's going to be rough on you."

I don't know whether he ever did try to go around and get anything.

I knew he couldn't go back to that motel, because I had called them and told them what had happened and that he was a phony. They were glad to hear he was gone because they were getting sick of the four-flusher.

I telephoned Cale Yarborough, "How's J.C. doing?"

"He's doing just fine. He is over in Timmonsville.

I told Cale what had happened and that we never expected to see the fake J.C. again.

Cale said, "You handled it just great. I'll tell J.C. Glad you got all your trophies back."

Don Brooks told me I should check in with the police so they could close their books on the case.

I talked to the police and the sheriff's department. One officer said, "That's all right. I'm just glad that you boys didn't get violent with him or anything. You could have been in trouble."

He said he was glad it had worked out and glad we had worked so fast to solve the matter because the guy would have left town and caused trouble for someone else.

I hope he learned his lesson. He was scared enough when I last saw him on the I-95 approach.

Curtis and Mary Francis, 1972.

CURTIS CRIDER, PRIVATE EYE

There was another time I was ripped off. Of course, that happens to other people, too many times.

I had a brand new set of cylinder heads and intake for my 427 cubic inch Ford engine. It was a new engine with pop-up pistons, all good stuff, 7,000 rpm, an engine which had just come out on the racing market.

After being off racing the Grand National car one weekend, I returned to the shop and discovered the cylinder heads were gone, had been stolen.

I was sick.

I narrowed it down to three suspects, people around town who knew what I had and might have stolen them.

I telephoned the three people separately and told each one the same thing, "Now, listen. I know you have my stuff. You can't use it. It won't work on any other engine unless you have the rest of the stuff to go with it and you can't get it.

"There are two things you can do. You can take the heads down to the river and throw them in or you can bring them back to me. If you bring them back, I won't be mad. I'm going to leave again Monday morning and I want those heads back up there by Sunday sundown."

Perhaps, on behalf of the innocent, I shouldn't have done it, but I told each one, privately, that I was sure he was the one who had done it. None of them protested very strongly, so maybe I don't owe any apology.

About 3 p.m. that Sunday, a fellow drove up in a Buick and said, "Curtis, I have your heads and the intake in the car. What do you want me to do with them?"

"Just take them right back there and put them exactly where you got them from."

I wouldn't even help him carry them in. He put them on the shelf where they were supposed to be.

Then I said, "Okay, I told you I wasn't going to hurt you and I won't be mad, because I really needed them back.

"Now, this is something else. This street out here is a city street and I know it's open to the public, but you have no relatives on this street and you have no reason to be on this street.

"Don't ever let me catch you in this neighborhood again. If my friends tell me you came back here, then I will get mad and I'll come looking for you."

He didn't argue. After all, I could have turned him over to the police as an admitted burglar.

Donnie Allison, Volusia County Speedway, 1973.

FINAL CHAPTER

There is a tendency today to compare the super-high salaries and income of major league athletes - auto racing, baseball, football and basketball - with the dollars earned by the comparable athletes who came along in the 1940s and '50s, and to declare that those of us in the latter group were born too soon.

As an auto racing driver in that earlier era, I have no regrets. I do not feel deprived. In our day, as today, there were the "haves" and the "have nots," those who were independents and those who had the factory-sponsored rides.

I do not feel that you can measure the success of a career or the quality of life strictly in terms of dollars earned. It is startling for a moment when you realize that the income of racing drivers of my era was a small percentage of the income of some of today's superstars.

But weigh, also, that the cost of living was much lower then for the average needs of life. Expensive technical equipment had not even been invented. Instead of the $70 a night motels at major interstate highway interchanges, we stayed at the mom and pop operated tourist cabins alongside two-lane blacktop highways named U.S. 1 and U.S. 40 and so on.

As country singing star Loretta Lynn once said, "We didn't know we were poor."

The Road To Daytona had many detours and several

potholes, but this man from Danville, Va., and the Carolinas made it to Daytona Beach and I raced on the World's Most Famous Beach and I raced on the Daytona International Speedway 2.5-mile trioval superspeedway, the Big D, the World Center of Auto Racing.

My goal was to do the very best I could with the equipment which was available to me, to try to be the best in my bracket.

Those of us who were independents did not begrudge those like Fireball Roberts, Curtis Turner, Little Joe Weatherly and Bob Welborn, who had the automobile factory-sponsored rides.

In my case, I can assure you, I enjoyed the hell out of what I was doing.

Both groups, the "haves" and the "have nots," got along well. One case in point, the 1964 World 600 at the Charlotte, N.C., Motor Speedway:

The factory teams used engines for practice and qualifying, then switched to race day engines. Lee Roy Yarbrough was a Mercury team driver and I was driving my own Mercury.

The deal was struck that Lee Roy would qualify his car, then give me his engine for my qualifying and it would be mine to keep.

Yarbrough qualified his car and the two crews worked feverishly to install his engine in my car. Then I qualified my car. Two cars qualified the same afternoon with the same engine! Then I drove the race with that engine.

There are many, many people to whom I owe thanks, for assistance, support and - most important - for their friendship through the years. It is not possible in these pages to thank them all, but they are none-the-less appreciated.

We followed The Road To Daytona and reached the goal. As they say in the Sunshine State, "When you get sand in your shoes, you will want to come back and stay." We did!

As you follow your own roads, may you reach your destinations.

God bless.

P.S.

Upon re-reading, I find that I have not mentioned my brother's wife Rosalie, or my son's wife Cheryl. There was no slight intended to them or to anyone else I may have missed.

My thanks also to Don O'Reilly, who transcribed and organized the book, to Steve McLachlin, who designed and illustrated it, to Katherine Keegan and Mike Arman of M. Arman Publishing, Inc., who keyed, ably proofread, typeset (11 point Bookman on 13 point leading, he says) and pasted it up, and to Arcata Printing, who printed it.

I'd like to especially thank all my friends and fellow racers, living or not, for this book. It is their story as well as mine: I just told it.

Photo Credits: Daytona International Speedway, T. Taylor Warren, Claudia Yon, Don Bock, Sam Satterwhite, Don O'Reilly, Sonny Deese, Jack Cansler, Bill Parry, Boyd Stanford, John H. Mobley, J. Carver Harris, Bob Verdun.

RACE RESULTS

MODIFIED & SPORTSMAN - 1958

1   Banjo Matthews, Asheville, N.C. . . . . '55 Ford (M)
2   Jimmy Thompson, Monroe, N.C. . . . . '49 Ford (M)
3   Glen Wood, Stuart, Va. . . . . '54 Ford (S)
4   Fireball Roberts, Daytona Beach, Fla. . . . . '55 Ford (M)
5   Paul Goldsmith, St. Clair Shores, Mich. . '50 Olds (M)
6   Bobby Johns, Miami, Fla. . . . . '37 Ford (S)
7   Vince Conrad, Kutztown, Pa. . . . . '37 Ford (S)
8   Frankie Schneider, Lambertville, N.J. . . . '37 Chevy (S)
9   Ralph Earnhardt, Kannapolis, N.C. . . . . . . '37 Ford (S)
10 Ned Jarrett, Newton, N.C. . . . . '38 Ford (S)
11 Chuck Thompson, Suncan, S.C. . . . . '49 Ford (M)
12 Ed Horn, Chalfont, Pa. . . . . '37 Ford (S)
13 **Curtis Crider, Charleston, S.C. . . . . '40 Ford (S)**
14 Chas. "Red" Farmer, Miami, Fla. . . . . . . '55 Chevy (M)
15 Al Graeber, Springfield, Pa. . . . . '37 Ford (S)
16 Ray Bennett, Jacksonville, Fla. . . . . '37 Ford (M)
17 Carl Burris, Leaksville, N.C. . . . . '36 Chevy (S)
18 Ralph Smith, Aberdeen, Md. . . . . '37 Ford (S)
19 David Ezell, Jacksonville, Fla. . . . . '38 Ford (M)
20 George Dunn, Raleigh, N.C. . . . . '37 Ford (S)
21 Dick Joslin, Orlando, Fla. . . . . '38 Chevy (M)
22 Ernie Gahan, Dover, N.H. . . . . '37 Ford (S)
23 Harry Hovis, St. Louis, Mo. . . . . '50 Chevy (M)
24 Wendell Scott, Danville, Va. . . . . '39 Ford (S)
25 Jack Hart, Chester, Pa. . . . . '37 Ford (S)

26	Harry Theobald, Norfolk, Va.	'37 Ford (S)
27	G.C. Spencer, Inman, S.C.	'36 Chevy (M)
28	Whip Mulligan, Denville, N.J.	'38 Ford (M)
29	A.L. King, St Louis, Mo.	'39 Ford (M)
30	Wilbur Flower, Orlando, Fla.	'37 Chevy (M)
31	Buren Skeen, Denton, N.C.	'37 Ford (S)
32	Doug Yates, Chapel Hill, N.C.	'37 Ford (S)
33	Rex White, Silver Spring, Md.	'37 Ford (M)
34	Dean Pelton, Silver Spring, Md.	'49 Ford (S)
35	Eddie Anders, Takoma Park, Md.	'38 Ford (M)
36	Larry Frank, Chicago, Ill.	'55 Buick (M)
37	Darel Dieringer, Indianapolis, Ind.	'37 Chevy (S)
38	Cotton Owens, Spartanburg, S.C.	'39 Plym. (M)
39	Speedy Thompson, Charlotte, N.C.	'37 Ford (M)
40	Bill Chevalier, Sayreville, N.J.	'40 Pont. (M)
41	Pete Kelley, Columbus, Ga.	'37 Ford (S)
42	Larry Flynn, Holly Hill, Fla.	'37 Ford (S)
43	Paul Gingrich, Mt. Jay, Pa.	'37 Ford (S)
44	Ernie Reeves, Hialeah, Fla.	'37 Ford (M)
45	Dink Widenhouse, Concord, N.C.	'37 Ford (M)
46	Herbie Tillman, Miami, Fla.	'38 Ford (M)
47	Billy Myers, Germantown, N.C.	'40 Ford (M)
48	Marvin Panch, Charlotte, N.C.	'39 Ford (M)
49	Sonny Palmer, Miami, Fla.	'36 Chevy (M)
50	Bob Reuther, Scottsboro, Ala.	'40 Chevy (M)
51	Jim Mairs, Wheaton, Md.	'40 Ford (S)
52	Ken Mariott, Baltimore, Md.	'37 Ford (M)
53	Curtis Turner, Roanoke, Va.	'36 Chevy (M)
54	Fred Schweikert, Miami, Fla.	'38 Chevy (M)
55	Rusty Kelley, Pontiac, Mich.	'37 Pont. (M)
56	Johnny Roberts, Baltimore, Md.	'37 Ford (M)
57	Phil Orr, Orlando, Fla.	'38 Plym. (M)
58	Paul Parker, Miami, Fla.,	'49 Ford (M)
59	Martin Handshaw, Maimi, Fla.	'52 Ford (M)
60	Jimmy Metzler, Parkerville, N.J.	'40 Ford (M)
61	Richard Freeman, Orlando, Fla.	'38 Plym. (M)
62	Jim Lerkins, Spencerport, N.Y.	'37 Ford (S)
63	William R. Gillelan, Plymouth, Mich.	'37 Dodge (M)
64	Lee Petty, Randleman, N.C.	'36 Chevy (M)
65	R.H. Ellis, Miami, Fla.	'50 Chevy (M)

66	Gwyn Staley, Burlington, N.C.	'37 Ford (M)
67	Allen Crowe, Phoenix, Ariz.	'38 Chevy (M)
68	Johnny Allen, Fayetteville, N.C..........	'37 Ford (S)
69	Bill Hess, Miami, Fla....................	'37 Ford (S)
70	Hooker Hood, Memphis, Tenn.........	'37 Chevy (M)
71	Chester Jones, Miami, Fla.	'37 Ford (M)

CONVERTIBLE - 1958

1	Curtis Turner, Roanoke, Va.	'58 Ford
2	Lee Petty, Randleman, N.C.	'57 Olds
3	Joe Weatherly, Norfolk, Va..................	'58 Ford
4	Buck Baker, Spartanburg, S.C.	'58 Chevy
5	Bob Pronger, Blue Island, Ill................	'57 Ford
6	Glen Wood, Stuart, Va.	'57 Ford
7	Tiny Lund, Harlan, Iowa..................	'57 Chevy
8	Gwyn Staley, Burlington, N.C.............	'57 Chevy
9	Ken Rush, High Point, N.C.	'57 Ford
10	Roz Howard, Macon, Ga.	'57 Chevy
11	Frankie Schneider, Lambertville, N.J.	'57 Chevy
12	Wilbur Rakestraw, Dallas, Ga.	'57 Ford
13	Bob Wellborn, Greensboro, N.C...........	'57 Chevy
14	Roy Tyner, Red Springs, N.C.	'58 Plym.
15	Possum Jones, Tampa, Fla................	'57 Chevy
16	Bill Morton, Church Hill, Tenn............	'57 Ford
17	Ken Hunley, Kingsport, Tenn.	'56 Ford
18	Ken Love, Chicago Heights, Ill.............	'57 Ford
19	J.V. Hamby, Columbia, S.C.	'56 Chevy
20	Marvin Panch, Charlotte, N.C.	'57 Ford
21	Browwnie King, Johnson City, Tenn.......	'57 Chevy
22	Carl Burris, Leaksville, N.C...............	'57 Chevy
23	Neil Castles, Charlotte, N.C...............	'56 Ford
24	Fireball Roberts, Daytona Beach, Fla.	'58 Ford
25	Bill Wimble, Lisbon, N.Y....................	'57 Ford
26	Shorty York, Mocksville, N.C.	'57 Mercury
27	Tim Flock, Atlanta, Ga.	'57 Mercury
28	Johnny Allen, Fayetteville, N.C.............	'57 Plym.
29	Ernie Walls, Indianapolis, Ind.	'58 Pontiac

Time: 1:37:24. Average speed, 98.563 MPH.
Fastest Qualifier: Lee Petty, average 133.829 MPH (new record)

THE LAST GO-ROUND - FEB. 23, 1958
GRAND NATIONAL

1	Paul Goldsmith	'58 Pont
2	Curtis Turner	'58 Ford
3	Jack Smith	'58 Pont
4	Joe Weatherly	'58 Ford
5	Gwyn Staley	'57 Chev
6	Lee Petty	'57 Olds
7	Buck Baker	'58 Chev
8	Eddie Pagan	'57 Ford
9	Fireball Roberts	'58 Buick
10	Cotton Owens	'57 Pont
11	Jim Thompson	'57 Pont
12	Dean Layfield	'58 Chev
13	Bill Morton	'57 Ford
14	Marvin Panch	'57 Ford
15	Charlie Stone	'57 Chev
16	Ward Towers	'57 Ford
17	Lloyd Ragon	'57 Ford
18	Cecil Wray	'57 Olds
19	Richard Foley	'56 Chev
20	Dick Bailey	'58 Pont
21	Joe Lee Johnson	'57 Chev
22	Carl Tyler	'57 Ford
23	Whitey Norman	'56 Ford
24	Buzz Woodward	'56 Ford
25	Eddie Skinner	'57 Ford
26	L.D. Austin	'56 Chev
27	Phil Orr	'58 Ford
28	Bob Walden	'57 Pont
29	Frankie Schneider	'57 Chev
30	Bill Myers	'57 Merc
31	Johnny Allen	'58 Plym
32	Bobby Lee	'58 Ford
33	Johnny Mackison	'57 Merc
34	Kenny Love	'57 Ford
35	Brownie King	'57 Chev

36	Banjo Mathews	'58 Chev
37	Bob Pronger	'57 Ford
38	Doug Yates	'58 Chev
39	Wilbur Rakestraw	'57 Ford
40	Dariel Dieringer	'57 Chev
41	Tiny Lund	'57 Chev
42	Bill Corley	'57 Ford
43	Dick Joslin	'57 Dodge
44	Frank Thompson	'57 Ford
45	Axle Anderson	'58 Merc
46	Tim Flock	'57 Merc
47	Carl Burris	'57 Chev
48	Speedy Thompson	'57 Chev
49	Benny Rakestraw	'57 Merc

100 MILE CONVERTIBLE RACE
DAYTONA, 1959

1	Lloyd "Shorty" Rollins, Corpus Christi, Tex.	'58 Ford
2	Marvin Panch, Charlotte, N.C.	'58 Ford
3	Richard Petty, Randleman, N.C.	'58 Ford
4	Glen Wood, Stuart, Va.	'58 Ford
5	Gene White, Marietta, Ga.	'57 Chevy
6	Larry Frank, Angier, N.C.	'58 Ford
7	Wilbur Rakestraw, Dallas, Ga.	'57 Ford
8	Joe Lee Johnson, Chattanooga, Tenn.	'57 Chevy
9	Jimmy Thompson, Monroe, N.C.	'57 Chevy
10	Bob Harkey, Charlotte, N.C.	'58 Chevy
11	Joe Eubanks, Spartanburg, S.C.	'58 Ford
12	Ken Rush, High Point, N.C.	'57 Mercury
13	Billy Carden, Atlanta, Ga.	'57 Mercury
14	Brownie King, Johnson City, Tenn.	'58 Chevy
15	Ben Benz, Far Rockaway, N.Y.	'57 Chevy
16	Pete Kelley, Macon, Ga.	'57 Chevy
17	George Green, Johnson City, Tenn.	'58 Chevy
18	Gober Sosebee, Atlanta, Ga.	'57 Chevy
19	Fred Hoff, Chicago, Ill.	'57 Ford
20	Paul Bass, Indianapolis, Ind.	'58 Edsel
21	Ken Marriott, Baltimore, Md.	'58 Ford

Time: 46 min., 26 sec. - Average 129.50 MPH.

100-MILE GRAND NATIONAL
DAYTONA - 1959

1	Bob Welborn, Greensboro, N.C.	'59 Chevy
2	Fred Wilson, Denver, Colo.	'59 T-Bird
3	Tom Pistone, Chicago, Ill.	'59 T-Bird
4	Joe Weatherly, Norfolk, Va.	'58 Chevy
5	Eduardo Dibos, Lima, Peru	'59 T-Bird
6	Cotton Owens, Spartanburg, S.C.	'58 Pontiac
7	Tiny Lund, Harlan, Iowa	'59 Chevy
8	Lee Petty, Randleman, N.C.	'59 Olds
9	Charlie Griffith, Chattanooga, Tenn.	'57 Pontiac
10	Rex White, Silver Spring, Md.	'59 Chevy
11	Johnny Beauchamp, Harlan, Iowa	'59 T-Bird
12	Bernie Hentges, Anoka, Minn.	'59 DeSoto
13	Dick Freeman, Dayton, Ohio	'59 Chevy
14	Dick Joslin, Orlando, Fla.	'57 Dodge
15	Bobby Johns, Miami, Fla.	'57 Chevy
16	Speedy Thompson, Charlotte, N.C.	'57 Chevy
17	Junior Johnson, Ronda, N.C.	'57 Ford
18	Raul Cilloniz, Lima, Peru	'58 Ford
19	Ken Johnson, Jamestown, N.Y.	'57 Ford
20	Jim Reed, Peekskill, N.Y.	'59 Chevy
21	Harold Smith, Dayton, Ohio	'59 Stude
22	Herman Beam, Johnson City, Tenn.	'57 Chevy
23	Carl Tyler, Marietta, Ga.	'57 Ford
24	Tim Flock, Atlanta, Ga.	'59 T-Bird
25	Roy Tyner, Red Springs, N.C.	'57 Chevy
26	Roscoe Thompson, Atlanta, Ga.	'57 Chevy
27	Jack Smith, Atlanta, Ga.	'59 Chevy
28	Buck Baker, Spartanburg, S.C.	'59 Chevy
29	Curtis Turner, Charlotte, N.C.	'59 T-Bird
30	Elmo Langley, Arlington, Va.	'57 Ford
31	Bob Duell, Frewsburg, N.Y.	'59 Ford
32	Jim McGuirk, Vero Beach, Fla.	'59 Pontiac
33	Fireball Roberts, Daytona Beach, Fla.	'59 Pontiac
34	Bob Potter, Duluth, Minn.	'59 Chevy
35	Bob Pronger, Blue Island, Ill.	'58 Ford
36	Bobby Rose, Inglewood, Calif.	'57 Chevy
37	Dick Foley, Montreal, Can.	'59 Chevy
38	L.D. Austin, Greenville, N.C.	'57 Chevy

200 MILE MODIFIED-SPORTSMAN RACE
FEB. 21, 1959

1   Banjo Mathews, Asheville, N.C............'56 Ford (M)
2   Perk Brown, Leaksville, N.C. .... '54 Ford (S)
3   Curtis Turner, Charlotte, N.C. .... '36 Chev (M)
4   Ed Lindsay, Baltimore, Md..............'40 Ford (M)
5   Lee Petty, Randleman, N.C. ....'50 Olds (M)
6   Al Tasnady, Vineland, N.J. .... '37 Chev (M)
7   Sonny Black, Montgomery, Ala. .... '37 Chev (M)
8   Bill Rafter, Buffalo, N.Y.................. '37 Chev (S)
9   Larry Flynn, Holly Hill, Fla. .... '37 Chev (S)
10 Bobby Johns, Miami, Fla............... '37 Ford (S)
11 Al Gorham, Miami, Fla.................. '37 Ford (S)
12 Dick Bailey, Grove City, Pa............ '38 Chev (M)
13 Harold Haberling, Phoenix, Ariz. .... '37 Plym (M)
14 Joe Kelly, Conshohocken, Pa. ....'37 Ford (M)
15 **Curtis Crider, Charleston, S.C.** .... **'55 Ford (S)**
16 G.C. Spencer, Inman, S.C. .... '36 Chev (M)
17 Larry Frank, Angier, N.C. .... '52 Plym (M)
18 Marvin Panch, Charlotte, N.C. .... 55 Ford (M)
19 Carl Burris, Leaksville, N.C............. '37 Chev (S)
20 Bill Wark, Harrington, N.J............... '37 Ford (S)
21 Stanley Parker, Maitland, Fla........... '37 Ford (S)
22 Spud Murphy, Lake Worth, Fla........ '56 Chev (M)
23 Red Farmer, Hialeah, Fla................ '37 Ford (S)
24 Harry Theobald, Norfolk, Va............'37 Ford (M)
25 Jimmy Thompson, Monroe, N.C. .... '49 Ford (S)
26 Hooker Hood, Memphis, Tenn.......... '50 Chev (M)
27 Eddie McDonald, Columbus, Ga........'37 Ford (M)
28 Shelton McNair, Plymouth, N.C........ '38 Chevy (S)
29 Wilbur Flower, Orlando, Fla. .... '50 Chevy (M)
30 Bob Gemenden, Franklinville, N.J. ......'37 Ford (M)
31 Speedy Thompson, Charlotte, N.C. ..... '37 Chevy (S)
32 Elmo Langley, Arlington, Va.............'49 Ford (M)
33 Chuck Mahoney, Jamestown, N.Y. ......'37 Ford (M)
34 Vince Conrad, Kutztown, Pa. .... '37 Ford (S)
35 Ken Shoemaker, Schenectady, N.Y....... '37 Ford (S)
36 Fireball Roberts, Daytona Beach, Fla. ...'55 Ford (M)
37 Glen Guthrie, Washington, D.C..........'40 Ford (M)

38	Ray Elby, St. Louis, Mo.	'37 Chevy (M)
39	Bill Hohman	'40 Ford (S)
40	Tom Gurley, Daytona Beach, Fla.	'50 Chevy (M)
41	James Hendrickson, Marrick, N.Y.	'39 Ford (M)
42	Johnny Roberts, Baltimore, Md.	'37 Ford (M)
43	Arthur Burt, Orlando, Fla.	'37 Plym (M)
44	David Ezell, Jacksonville, Fla.	'37 Ford (S)
45	Dick Joslin, Orlando, Fla.	'37 Dodge (M)
46	Bobby Albert, White Plains, N.Y.	'37 Ford (M)
47	Cam Gagliardi, Lockport, N.Y.	'39 Ford (S)
48	Rex White, Silver Spring, Md.	'40 Ford (M)
49	Charlie Cregar, Trenton, N.J.	'39 Chevy (M)
50	Wendell Scott, Danville, Va.	'49 Ford (S)

25-MILE LATE MODEL CONSOLATION RACE
FEB. 21, 1959

1	Jack Smith, Atlanta, Ga.	'59 Chevy Impala
2	Curtis Turner, Charlotte, N.C.	'59 T-Bird
3	Tim Flock, Atlanta, Ga.	'59 T-Bird
4	Dick Foley, Montreal, Canada	'59 Chevy Impala
5	Bob Potter, Duluth, Minn.	'59 Chevy
6	Fireball Roberts, Daytona Beach, Fla.	'59 Pontiac
7	Bob Pronger, Blue Island, Ill.	'58 Ford
8	Elmo Langley, Arlington, Va.	'57 Ford
9	Herman Beam, Johnson City, Tenn.	'57 Chevy
10	Harold Smith, Dayton, Ohio	'59 Studebaker
11	Bob Duell, Frewsburg, N.Y.	'59 Ford
12	Carl Tyler, Marietta, Ga.	'57 Ford
13	Jim McGuirk, Vero Beach, Fla.	'59 Pontiac
14	Buck Baker, Charlotte, N.C.	'59 Chevy Impala
15	Bobby Rose, Inglewood, Calif.	'57 Chevy

To order more copies of **The Road To Daytona**, send $7.95 plus $1.00 for postage and handling to:

Curtis W. Crider
1077 Roberts St.
Ormond Beach, FL 32074

Thank You!